BRAIN GAMES™

Consultant: Elkhonon Goldberg, Ph.D.

Publications International, Ltd.

Elkhonon Goldberg, Ph.D., ABPP/ABCN, (consultant) is a clinical professor of neurology at New York University School of Medicine, a diplomate of the American Board of Professional Psychology/American Board of Clinical Neuropsychology, and director of The East-West Science and Education Foundation. Dr. Goldberg created the Manhattan-based Cognitive Enhancement Program, a fitness center for the brain, and he is author of the international best-selling books *The Wisdom Paradox: How Your Mind Can Grow as Your Brain Grows Older* and *The Executive Brain: Frontal Lobes and the Civilized Mind.*

Contributing Writers: Elkhonon Goldberg, Ph.D., Holli Fort

Puzzlers: Myles Callum, Barry Clarke, Kelly Clark, Jeanette Dall, Mark Danna, Josie Faulkner, Connie Formby, Erich Friedman, Peter Grabarchuk, Serhiy Grabarchuk, Dave Green, Ray Hamel, Luke Haward, Dick Hess, Marilynn Huret, Lloyd King, David Millar, Alan Olschwang, Timothy Parker, Ellen F. Pill, Ph.D., Dave Roberts, Marilyn Roberts, Stephen Ryder, Steve Schaefer, Paul Seaburn, Terry Stickels, Fraser Simpson, Shavan R. Spears, Howard Tomlinson

Additional Puzzle Editing: Fraser Simpson

Illustrators: Nicole H. Lee, Shozen Jay Sato, Shavan R. Spears

Back Cover Puzzles: Connie Formby, Steve Schaefer

Brain Games is a trademark of Publications International, Ltd.

ISBN-13: 978-1-4127-1598-0
ISBN-10: 1-4127-1598-9

Manufactured in China.

8 7 6 5 4 3 2 1

CONTENTS

BRAIN FITNESS

Your mind is your most important asset—more important than your house, your bank account, and your stock portfolio. You insure your house and work hard to pad your bank account. But what can you do to sharpen your mind and protect it from decline? With the baby boomer generation getting on in years, an increasing number of people are asking this question. Modern-day science provides a clear answer: Protect your mind by protecting your brain. To understand this relationship further, we turn to cutting-edge research.

Protect and Enhance Your Brainpower

Modern-day neuroscience has established that our brain is a far more plastic organ than was previously thought. In the past it was believed that an adult brain can only lose nerve cells (neurons) and cannot acquire new ones. Today we know that new neurons—and new connections between neurons—continue to develop throughout our lives, even well into advanced age. This process is called *neuroplasticity*. Thanks to recent scientific discoveries, we also know that we can harness the powers of neuroplasticity in protecting and even enhancing our minds at every stage of life—including our advanced years.

How can we harness neuroplasticity to help protect and enhance our mental powers? Recent scientific research demonstrates that the brain responds to mental stimulation much like muscles respond to physical exercise. In other words, you

have to give your brain a workout. The more vigorous and diverse your mental life—and the more you welcome mental challenges—the more you will stimulate the growth of new neurons and new connections between them. Furthermore, the *nature* of your mental activities influences *where* in the brain this growth takes place. The brain is a very complex organ with different parts in charge of different mental functions. Thus, different cognitive challenges exercise different components of the brain.

How do we know this? We've learned this by experiments created from real-life circumstances and *neuroimaging*, the high-resolution technologies that allow scientists to study brain structure and function with amazing precision. Some say that these technologies have done for our understanding of the brain what the invention of the telescope has done for our understanding of the planetary systems. Thanks to these technologies, particularly MRI (magnetic resonance imaging), we know that certain parts of the brain exhibit an increased size in those who use these parts of the brain more than most people. For example, researchers found that hippocampi, the parts of the brain critical for spatial memory, were larger than usual in London cab drivers who have to navigate and remember complex routes in a huge city. Studies revealed that the so-called Heschl's gyrus, a part of the temporal lobe of the brain involved in processing music, is larger in professional musicians than in musically untrained people. And the angular gyrus, the part of the brain involved in language, proved to be larger in bilingual individuals than in those who speak only one language.

What is particularly important—the size of the effect, the extent to which the part of the brain was enlarged—was di-

rectly related to the *amount of time* each person spent in the activities that rely on the part of the brain in question. For instance, the hippocampal size was directly related to the number of years the cab driver spent on the job, and the size of Heschl's gyrus was associated with the amount of time a musician devoted to practicing a musical instrument. This shows that cognitive activity directly influences the structures of the brain by stimulating the effects of neuroplasticity in these structures, since the enlargement of brain regions implies a greater than usual number of cells or connections between them. The impact of cognitive activity on the brain can be great enough to result in an actual increase in its size! Indeed, different parts of the brain benefit directly from certain activities, and the effect can be quite specific.

Diversify Your Mental Workout

It is also true that any more or less complex cognitive function—be it memory, attention, perception, decision making, or problem solving—relies on a whole network of brain regions rather than on a single region. Therefore, any relatively complex mental challenge will engage more than one part of the brain, yet no single mental activity will engage the whole brain.

This is why the diversity of your mental life is key to your overall brain health. The more vigorous and varied your cognitive challenges, the more efficiently and effectively they'll protect your mind from decline. To return to the workout analogy: Imagine a physical gym. No single exercise machine will make you physically fit. Instead, you need a balanced and diverse workout regime.

You have probably always assumed that crossword puzzles and sudoku are good for you, and they are. But your cognitive workout will benefit more from a greater variety of exercises, particularly if these exercises have been selected with some knowledge of how the brain works.

The puzzle selection for *Brain Games*™ has been guided by these considerations—with knowledge of the brain and the roles played by its different parts in the overall orchestra of your mental life. We aimed to assemble as wide a range of puzzles as possible in order to offer the brain a full workout.

There is no single magic pill to protect or enhance your mind, but vigorous, regular, and diverse mental activity is the closest thing to it. Research indicates that people engaged in mental activities as a result of their education and vocation are less likely to develop dementia as they age. In fact, many of these people demonstrate impressive mental alertness well into their eighties and nineties.

What's more, the pill does not have to be bitter. You can engage in activities that are both good for your brain *and* fun. Different kinds of puzzles engage different aspects of your mind, and you can assemble them all into a cognitive workout regime. Variety is the name of the game—that's the whole idea! In any single cognitive workout session, have fun by mixing puzzles of different kinds. This book offers you enough puzzle variety to make this possible.

Welcome challenging puzzles, instead of feeling intimidated by them. Never give up! To be effective as a mental workout, the puzzles should not be too easy or too difficult. An overly easy puzzle will not stimulate your brain, just as a leisurely walk in the park is not an efficient way to condition your heart. You need mental exertion. On the other hand, an overly difficult puzzle will just frustrate and discourage you from moving forward. So it is important to find the "challenge zone" that is appropriate for you. This may vary from person to person and from puzzle to puzzle. Here too, the gym analogy applies. Different people will benefit most from different exercise machines and from different levels of resistance and weights.

With this in mind, we have tried to offer a range of difficulty for every puzzle type. Try different puzzles to find the starting level appropriate to you. And before you know it, your puzzle-cracking ability will improve, your confidence will grow, and this will be a source of reassurance, satisfaction, and even pride.

Have Fun While Stretching Your Mind

The important thing is to have fun while doing something good for you. Puzzles can be engaging, absorbing, and even addictive. An increasing number of people make regular physical exercise part of their daily routines and miss it when circumstances prevent them from exercising. These habitual gym-goers know that strenuous effort is something to look forward to, not to avoid. Similarly, you will strengthen your mental muscle by actively challenging it. Don't put the puzzle book down when the solution is not immediately apparent. By testing your mind you will discover the joy of a particular kind of accomplishment: watching your mental powers grow. You must have the feeling of mental effort and exertion in order to exercise your brain.

This brings us to the next issue. While all puzzles are good for you, the degree of their effectiveness as brain conditioners is not the same. Some puzzles only test your knowledge of facts. Such puzzles may be enjoyable and useful to a degree, but they're not as useful in conditioning your brain as the puzzles that require you to transform and manipulate information or do something with it by logic, multistep inference, mental rotation, planning, and so on. The latter puzzles are more likely to give you the feeling of mental exertion, of "stretching your mind," and they are also better for your brain health. You can use this feeling as a useful, though inexact, assessment of a puzzle's effectiveness as a brain conditioner.

Try to select puzzles in a way that complements, rather than duplicates, your job-related activities. If your profession involves dealing with words (e.g., an English teacher), try to emphasize spatial puzzles. If you are an engineer dealing with diagrams, focus on verbal puzzles. If your job is relatively devoid of mental challenges of any kind, mix several types of puzzles in equal proportions.

Cognitive decline frequently sets in with aging. It often affects certain kinds of memory and certain aspects of attention and decision making. So it is particularly important to introduce cognitive exercise into your lifestyle as you age to counteract any possible cognitive decline. But cognitive exercise is also important for the young and the middle-aged. We live in a world that depends increasingly on the brain more than on the brawn. It is important to be sharp in order to get ahead in your career and to remain at the top of your game.

How frequently should you exercise your mind and for how long? Think in terms of an ongoing lifestyle change and not just a short-term commitment. Regularity is key, perhaps a few times a week for 30 to 45 minutes at a time. We've tried to make this easier by offering a whole series of *Brain Games*™ books. You can carry these puzzle books—your "cognitive workout gym"—in your briefcase, backpack, or shopping bag. Our puzzles are intended to be fun, so feel free to fit them into your lifestyle in a way that enhances rather than disrupts it. Research shows that even a relatively brief regimen of vigorous cognitive activity often produces perceptible and lasting effects. But as with physical exercise, the results are best when cognitive exercise becomes a lifelong habit.

To help you gauge your progress, we have included two self-assessment questionnaires: one near the beginning of the book and one near the end. The questionnaires will guide you in rating your various cognitive abilities and any change that you may experience as a result of do-

ing puzzles. Try to be as objective as possible when you fill out the questionnaires. Improving your cognitive skills in real-life situations is the most important practical outcome of exercising your mind, and you are in the best position to note such improvement and to decide whether or not it has taken place.

Now that you're aware of the great mental workout that awaits you in this book, we hope that you'll approach these puzzles with a sense of fun. If you have always been a puzzle fan, we offer a great rationale for indulging your passion! You have not been wasting your time by cracking challenging puzzles—far from it; you have been training and improving your mind.

So, whether you are a new or seasoned puzzle-solver, enjoy your brain workout and get smarter as you go!

ASSESS YOUR BRAIN

You are about to do something very smart: embark on a set of exercises to improve the way your mind works. The puzzles assembled in this book are fun and they have been selected to hone your memory, attention, problem-solving, and other important mental skills. So before you begin, we would like you to fill out a brief questionnaire. It is for your own benefit, so you know how your mind worked before you challenged it with our exercises. This will allow you to decide in the future if any change in your mental performance has taken place and in what areas.

The questions below are designed to test your skills in the areas of memory, problem-solving, creative thinking, attention, language, and more. Please take a moment to think about your answers and rate your responses on a 5-point scale, where 5 equals "excellent" and 1 equals "very poor." Then tally up your scores, and go to the categories at the bottom of the next page to see how you did.

1. You get a new cell phone. How long does it take you to remember the number? Give yourself a 1 if you have to check the phone every time you want to give out the number and a 5 if you know it by heart the next day.

1   2   3   4   5

2. How good are you at remembering where you put things? Give yourself a 5 if you never lose anything but a 1 if you have to search for the keys every time you want to leave the house.

1   2   3   4   5

3. You have a busy work day that you've carefully planned around a doctor's appointment. At the last minute, the doctor's office calls and asks you to reschedule your appointment from afternoon to morning. How good are you at juggling your plans to accommodate this change?

1   2   3   4   5

4. You're taking a trip back to your hometown and have several old friends to see, as well as old haunts to visit. You'll only be there for three days. How good are you at planning your visit so you can accomplish everything?

1   2   3   4   5

5. A friend takes you to a movie, and the next morning a curious coworker wants to hear the plot in depth. How good are you at remembering all the details?

1   2   3   4   5

6. Consider this scenario: You're brokering an agreement between two parties (could be anything from a business merger to making peace between feuding siblings), and both parties keep changing their demands. How good are you at adapting to the changing situation?

1   2   3   4   5

7. You're cooking a big meal for a family celebration. Say you have to cook everything—appetizers, entrees, sides, and desserts—all on the same day. How good are you at planning out each recipe so that everything is done and you can sit down and enjoy the meal with your family?

1   2   3   4   5

8. In an emotionally charged situation (for example, when you're giving a toast), can you usually come up with the right words to describe your feelings?

1   2   3   4   5

9. You and five friends have made a vow to always spend a certain amount of money on each other for holiday gifts. How good are you at calculating the prices of things in your head to make sure you spend the right amount of money?

1   2   3   4   5

10. You're moving, and you have to coordinate all the details of packing, hiring movers, cutting off and setting up utilities, and a hundred other small details. How good are you at planning out this complex situation?

1   2   3   4   5

10–25 Points: Are You Ready to Make a Change?

Remember, it's never too late to improve your brain health! A great way to start is to work puzzles each day, and you've taken the first step by buying this book. Choose a different type of puzzle each day, or do a variety of them to help strengthen memory, focus attention, and improve logic and problem-solving.

26–40 Points: Building Your Mental Muscles

You're no mental slouch, but there's always room to sharpen your mind! Choose puzzles that will challenge you, especially the types of puzzles you might not like as much or wouldn't normally do. Remember, doing a puzzle can be the mental equivalent of doing lunges or squats: While they might not be your first choice of activities, you'll definitely like the results!

41–50 Points: View from the Top

Congratulations! You're keeping your brain in tip-top shape. To maintain this level of mental fitness, keep challenging yourself by working puzzles every day. Like the rest of the body's muscles, your mental strength can decline if you don't use it. So choose to keep your brain supple and strong. You're at the summit, now you just have to stay to enjoy the view!

FLIPPING THE SWITCH

Ace It!

LANGUAGE ATTENTION VISUAL SEARCH

Ignoring spaces and punctuation, how many occurrences of the consecutive letters A-C-E can you find in the paragraph below?

Grace, a certified hypochondriac, envisioned a day when she could go anyplace without a sick look on her face. Grace aced college but didn't get an MBA, ceasing her studies when she met Chase, a cerebral student of crustaceans who loved to look at her face and embrace her curvaceous figure. Being a recovering hypochondriac enabled Chase to relate to Grace, and he helped her recover by sharing his favorite placebo.

Math Grid

LOGIC COMPUTATION

Fill each square in the grid with a digit from 1 through 9. When the numbers in each row are added, you should arrive at the total in the right-hand column. When the numbers in each column are added, you should arrive at the total on the bottom line. The numbers in each diagonal must add up to the totals in the upper and lower right corners.

			7
2		1	11
5			12
		1	11
9	20	5	7

Answers on page 171.

Tut's Tomb

Those gold bars at the center of the maze are worth millions—but they're encased in the tomb. Can you find the only way to the riches?

Wacky Wordy

CREATIVE THINKING   LANGUAGE

Can you "read" the phrase below?

PLAY

THERIM

Answers on page 171.

Sudoku

Use deductive logic to complete the grid so that each row, each column, and each 3×3 box contains the numbers 1 through 9 in some order. The solution is unique.

	2		1		5		3	
7	4				6			
9	1							2
6	8	4	9				2	1
	7	2				9	5	
5	9				2	3	6	4
1							9	3
			3				8	6
	3		8		1		4	

Trivia on the Brain

The retina of the eye is the only part of the central nervous system that can be seen from outside of the body, but you have to look directly through the pupil to see it.

Answers on page 171.

Name Calling

Decipher the encoded word in the quip below using the numbers and letters on the phone pad. Remember that each number can stand for 3 or 4 possible letters.

He who blows his stack only adds to the 9–6–7–5–3'–7 pollution.

1	2 ABC	3 DEF
4 GHI	5 JKL	6 MNO
7 PQRS	8 TUV	9 WXYZ
	0	

Hinky Pinky

The clues below lead to a 2-word answer that rhymes, such as Big Pig or Stable Table. The numbers in parentheses after the clues give the number of syllables in each word.

1. Correct elevation (1): __ __ __ __ __   __ __ __ __ __ __

2. Depart from Adam's wife (1): __ __ __ __ __   __ __ __

3. Unsettled a sentry (1): __ __ __ __ __ __   __ __ __ __ __

4. Rollaway bed on a millionaire's boat (1): __ __ __ __ __   __ __ __

5. Old mother with a bare cupboard sobbed loudly (2): __ __ __ __ __ __ __ __

__ __ __ __ __ __ __ __ __ __

Answers on page 171.

Acrostic Anagram

Unscramble the words below, then transfer the corresponding letters to the grid. When you're finished, you'll be rewarded with a quote by Agnes Repplier.

1 D	2 H	3 K	4 B	5 C	6 F		7 J	8 B	9 L		10 A (C)	11 J	12 A (N)	13 G	14 I	15 I		16 I	17 J
18 B	19 K	20 D	21 F	22 G	23 G	24 G		25 G		26 L	27 I	28 C	29 F	30 A (A)	31 K	32 J	33 C		34 I
35 A (B)	36 B	37 L	38 J	39 E	40 A (I)	41 L	42 B		43 E	44 E	45 E		46 I	47 K	48 H	49 D		50 B	51 L
52 H	53 E		54 G	55 D		56 D	57 H	58 C		59 E	60 E	61 J		62 H	63 G		64 F	65 I	66 C
67 D	68 G	69 B	70 K	71 F	72 L	73 J	74 B	75 B										

A. 10 30 35 40 12
   C A B I N
   A C I N B

B. 36 42 50 4 8 74 75 69 18
   _ _ _ _ _ _ _ _ _
   M O P S Y C H I N

C. 5 33 66 58 28
   _ _ _ _ _
   E E L V L

D. 56 49 1 67 55 20
   _ _ _ _ _ _
   N P I Y T G

E. 59 43 44 53 45 60 39
   _ _ _ _ _ _ _
   A A W R D H E

F. 29 6 64 71 21
   _ _ _ _ _
   C A P N E

G. 63 22 13 25 68 54 23 24
   _ _ _ _ _ _ _ _
   I A L Z N F E I

H. 52 57 62 48 2
   _ H _ _ _
   E H C O R

I. 27 46 65 34 15 14 16
   _ _ _ _ _ _ _
   O I A T A V R

J. 7 17 11 38 73 32 61
   _ _ _ _ _ _ _
   L I R Y W E A

K. 31 19 3 70 47
   _ _ _ _ _
   O B O E Z

L. 9 51 41 26 37 72
   _ _ _ P _ _
   T P U U T O

Answers on page 171.

15

At the Zoo

ATTENTION   LANGUAGE   VISUAL SEARCH

Every word listed is contained within the group of letters below. The words can be found in a straight line horizontally, vertically, or diagonally. The words can be read backward or forward.

```
R A E B Z G A Z E L L E G
E G S O R E C O N I H R O
H I P P O P O T A M U S R
T R L A J X E A O E U N I
N A I W N A N N N A A L
A F O O G D K Y G E N K L
P F N L T E A T L U Y E A
E E E F Y W A C A M I H D
R E G I T E L E P H A N T
```

BEAR	HIPPOPOTAMUS	PANTHER
EAGLE	HYENA	PENGUIN
ELEPHANT	LION	RHINOCEROS
GAZELLE	LYNX	SNAKE
GIRAFFE	MACAW	TIGER
GNU	MONKEY	WOLF
GORILLA	PANDA	

Answers on page 171.

Sudoku

LOGIC

Use deductive logic to complete the grid so that each row, each column, and each 3×3 box contains the numbers 1 through 9 in some order. The solution is unique.

	8					7		
9		5	8	7	4		1	
3	7	4					5	8
			3		6		7	2
		3				8		
1	4		7		8			
4	1					3	2	5
	3		4	5	2	1		7
		6					8	

Word Ladders

PLANNING   LANGUAGE

Change just 1 letter on each line to go from the top word to the bottom word. Do not change the order of the letters. You must have a common English word at each step.

1. FOND

_____

_____ the back legs

_____

_____ some are magic

_____

_____ a beverage notably produced in France and California

_____

MINT

2. HOPE

_____ you can dig one

_____

_____ repulsive

_____

_____ fruit that is just right to eat

ROPE

Answers on page 171.

Crossword for Dummies

GENERAL KNOWLEDGE   LANGUAGE

ACROSS

1. Prima donna
5. Chemical banned in the U.S. in 1972
8. Male clotheshorses
12. Surpassed
14. Dog in "Garfield"
15. One who works with a dummy
17. Superlative ending
18. Bankbook increase (abbr.)
19. Wrist bones
20. Slow run
21. ___ Moines, Iowa
22. Cry from a roller coaster
25. Stage signal
26. Shriner's topper
29. Game played with a dummy
33. Sporty Pontiac model
34. Start for Quentin or Diego
35. Skillet metal
36. Long-jawed fish
37. Mai ___
39. Western African nation
42. Big donating org.
43. Belittle, slangily
46. It involves putting a dummy in a car
49. Not fat
50. School fundraiser, often
51. Be misanthropic
52. Org. with many examiners
53. Kind of school

DOWN

1. White bird
2. Currier's partner
3. Air duct
4. Gallery showing
5. "Nothing ___!" ("No way!")
6. Oaf
7. Potential fight ender (abbr.)
8. Sports no-nos
9. One-eyed Norse god
10. Leaning Tower city
11. Rests
13. Tony Orlando and Dawn, e.g.
16. Unusually different
20. Fighter plane
21. Name
22. Move back and forth, as a finger
23. Simple abode
24. Prefix with system
25. "The Situation Room" network
26. HST's predecessor
27. Self-importance
28. School of Buddhism
30. Bartender on "The Love Boat"
31. Boat mover
32. Number on a grandfather clock
36. Garden statue
37. Pieces of work
38. Stomach trouble
39. Knife cut

40. ___ hoop
41. Fighting
42. Former host of "The Tonight Show"
43. Letter opener

44. Remote getaway
45. Put one's foot down?
47. Baseball stat
48. One-third of a Tbsp.

1	2	3	4		5	6	7		8	9	10	11
12				13					14			
15							16					
17				18				19				
			20				21					
22	23	24				25				26	27	28
29				30	31			32				
33				34				35				
			36			37	38					
39	40	41				42			43	44	45	
46				47				48				
49				50								
51				52				53				

Trivia on the Brain
Humans have the largest brains in relation
to their body size of any animal on the planet.

Answers on page 172.

Name Calling

ATTENTION   **VISUAL SEARCH**

Decipher the encoded word in the quip below using the numbers and letters on the phone pad. Remember that each number can stand for 3 or 4 possible letters.

As soon as you have graduated from the school of experience, someone adds a new 2–6–8–7–7–3.

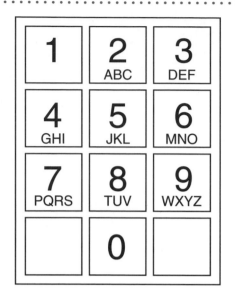

Three-Letter Anagrams

LANGUAGE

Fill in the blanks in each sentence below with words that are anagrams (rearrangements) of one another.

1. She _____ eat the _____ casserole.

2. Sam wanted to use the _____, _____ the drain was clogged.

3. Mom _____ angry when she _____ the mess.

4. The tourist asked, " _____ knows _____ to speak French?"

5. The truck could _____ carry a _____ of bricks.

Answers on page 172.

Big Top Code-doku

Solve this puzzle just as you do a sudoku. Use deductive logic to complete the grid so that each row, each column, and each 3×3 box contains 1 of the letters of the anagram WORD SLAVE. The solution is unique. When you have completed the puzzle, the shaded squares will form a hidden message read top to bottom from left to right.

								E
		E	O	L	D		A	R
						A	R	
O			D					
	W	S			R	O		
	A	V		E				
A				V			W	O
			W			D		
	L					E		

Hidden message: _____

Wacky Wordy

Can you "read" the phrase below?

THEBLUEFACE

Answers on page 172.

Hinky Pinky

The clues below lead to a 2-word answer that rhymes, such as Big Pig or Stable Table. The number in parentheses after each clue gives the number of syllables in each word of the answer. As a bonus, can you find the theme of this puzzle?

1. Hock a baby deer (1): __ __ __ __   __ __ __ __

2. Intelligent Lancelot, for one (1): __ __ __ __ __ __   __ __ __ __ __ __

3. Annoying inconvenience in a place with a moat (2): __ __ __ __ __ __

__ __ __ __ __ __

4. Nasty head of the hive (1): __ __ __ __   __ __ __ __ __

5. Take along CNN talk show host Larry (1): __ __ __ __ __   __ __ __ __

Theme: _____

All Hands on Deck

Amy has 5 hands, Betty has 4 hands, and Carol has 2 hands, yet they had no problem when it was time to join hands and form a circle. Why not?

Trivia on the Brain
The first cervical dorsal spinal nerve and dorsal root ganglia, which bring sensory information into the brain and spinal cord, are missing in 50 percent of all people.

Answers on page 172.

Screwprint: Upside Down?

SPATIAL VISUALIZATION   **ATTENTION**   **LOGIC**

Two identical screws are placed on a sheet of paper as shown. If the screws are rolled into the center of the paper, what pattern will they make?

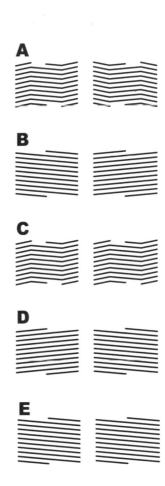

A

B

C

D

E

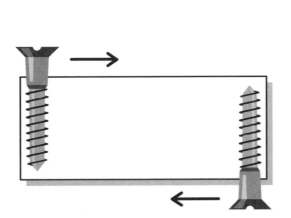

Answer on page 172.

Crossword Snack

Solve the crossword clues to fill in this 5×5 word square.

ACROSS

1. Tropical nut
6. Join forces
7. Playground retort
8. Comic strip by Greg Evans
9. Uptight

DOWN

1. Constructed
2. Follow
3. Mythological giant
4. Some jackets or collars
5. Sierra ___

1	2	3	4	5
6				
7				
8				
9				

Wacky Wordy

Can you "read" the phrase below?

ANOTHERONETHING

Answers on page 172.

Acrostic Anagram

Unscramble the words below, then transfer the corresponding letters to the grid. When you're finished, you'll be rewarded with a quote by Jules Renard.

1 D	2 C	3 D	4 E	5 C	6 K	7 J		8 G	9 F		10 I	11 F	12 A E		13 F	14 A N	15 B	16 E	
17 D	18 I	19 E	20 C	21 K	22 H	23 J	24 A I	25 K	26 G		27 B	28 L	29 G	30 B	31 G		32 E	33 G	
34 I	35 H	36 J		37 F	38 C	39 K	40 L	41 K	42 I	43 B	44 K	45 D		46 D	47 F	48 K		49 E	50 A I
51 A D	52 J	53 E	54 C	55 F	56 B	57 E	58 C		59 L	60 B		61 L	62 A O	63 C		64 J	65 I	66 H	67 I
	68 G	69 I		70 G	71 H	72 N	73 H	74 B											

A. 24 62 51 50 14 12
I O D I N E
NIEIDO

B. 60 15 56 27 43 30 74
_ _ _ _ _ _ _
LFERYOW

C. 20 54 2 5 38 63 58
_ _ _ _ _ _ _
UUFRSOI

D. 1 3 45 17 46
_ _ _ _ _
SYPWI

E. 53 19 57 32 4 49 16
_ _ _ _ _ _ _
NCUYOTR

F. 9 37 11 13 47 55
_ _ H _ _ _
CSOLOH

G. 26 33 70 8 68 31 29
_ _ _ _ _ _ _
ENOIMNE

H. 22 35 71 66 73
_ N _ _ _
NSOER

I. 10 34 18 67 65 42 69
_ _ _ _ _ D _
ROONDTA

J. 23 52 36 7 64
_ _ _ _ _
GIEES

K. 44 21 48 39 41 25 6
_ _ _ _ _ _ _
IUNRENO

L. 40 28 59 72 61
_ _ _ _ _
NIYSH

Answers on page 172.

Sudoku

Use deductive logic to complete the grid so that each row, each column, and each 3×3 box contains the numbers 1 through 9 in some order. The solution is unique.

8	2					6		
1	5		7					9
		9						8
6	8	1	5		7		9	4
	9		1		4		8	
3	4		9		8	1	7	6
5						8		
2					6		1	3
		4					6	2

Wacky Wordy

Can you "read" the phrase below?

MT

PROMISE

PROMISE

PROMISE

Answers on page 172.

Squarely Put Together

Fit the 5 pieces below together to form a square.

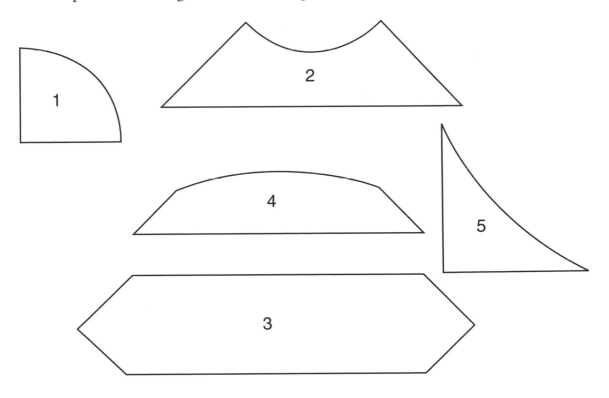

Wacky Wordy

Can you "read" the phrase below?

THE WEATHER

THE WHETHER

Answers on page 172.

Name Calling

Decipher the encoded word in the quip below using the numbers and letters on the phone pad. Remember that each number can stand for 3 or 4 possible letters.

It is difficult to make predictions, especially about the 3–8–8–8–7–3.

1	2 ABC	3 DEF
4 GHI	5 JKL	6 MNO
7 PQRS	8 TUV	9 WXYZ
	0	

Word Ladders

Change just 1 letter on each line to go from the top word to the bottom word. Do not change the order of the letters. You must have a common English word at each step.

1. PEACH

_____ educate

_____ shore

_____

LEECH

2. SHOW

_____ not quick

_____

_____ do farm work

_____

_____ an object used in a theatrical production

DROP

Answers on page 172.

Hinky Pinky

The clues below lead to a 2-word answer that rhymes, such as Big Pig or Stable Table. The number in parentheses after each clue gives the number of syllables in each word of the answer. Can you figure out what the theme of this puzzle is?

1. Bisected a cherry stone (1): _ _ _ _ _ _ _ _

2. Tidy avenue (1): _ _ _ _ _ _ _ _ _ _

3. Constructed a leg pole for a clown (1): _ _ _ _ _ _ _ _ _ _

4. Close-in-score boxing match (1): _ _ _ _ _ _ _ _ _ _

5. One more than 7 in a row (1): _ _ _ _ _

_ _ _ _ _ _ _

Theme: _____

Trivia on the Brain

Many people believe that Albert Einstein had a huge brain, but this is false. He was actually a small person with a smaller than average size brain. Einstein's great intelligence came from the huge number of connections that were formed between his many brain cells, which happened every time he learned something new.

Answers on page 173.

Circle Maze

Can you find your way to the center of this maze?

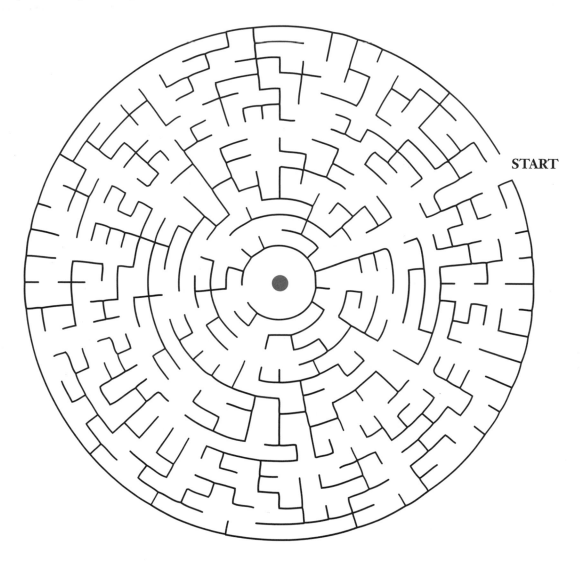

START

Answer on page 173.

Weather Word Search

Every word listed is contained within the group of letters below. The words can be found in a straight line horizontally, vertically, or diagonally. The words can be read backward or forward.

CLOUD

COLD

FAIR

FOG

FROST

HOT

HUMID

ICE

LIGHTNING

RAIN

SLEET

SNOW

STORM

SUNSHINE

TORNADO

WIND

```
F  M  D  S  L  E  E  T  F
A  R  L  U  N  T  T  O  A
H  E  O  N  W  O  H  D  I
C  D  C  S  C  O  W  A  R
L  I  G  H  T  N  I  N  G
O  M  O  I  N  I  N  R  O
U  U  O  N  C  A  D  O  F
D  H  R  E  M  R  O  T  S
```

Answers on page 173.

Crossword Snack

Enjoy a quick mental workout? This one's for you. Answer the clues to fill the crossword square with just 10 words.

ACROSS

1. Drabs partner
6. Internet search engine
7. The Donald's first
8. At no time
9. Sharon of "Cagney & Lacey"

DOWN

1. "___ is easy. Comedy is hard."
2. Bolero composer
3. "___ a dream . . ."
4. Skeleton parts
5. Flies high

Don't Lose Your Head!

Can you "read" the title below?

$$\text{HULLUW}$$
$$\ddot{\text{U}}$$

Answers on page 173.

Cool Café

In the Cool Café, the waiter has written down his orders incorrectly. Each item is in the correct column, but only one entry in each column is correctly positioned. Can you give the surname, drink, and number of sugar lumps for each?

	Surname	Drink	Sugar lumps
1	Aviary	tea	0
2	Bloggs	coffee	1
3	Crumple	latte	2
4	Dribble	mocha	3

1. The latte or the coffee was ordered with either 0 or 1 sugar.

2. Second to receive their order is Aviary, who has neither 1 nor 3 sugars and did not order a latte.

3. Just after Aviary is neither Bloggs nor Dribble, but whoever it is receives 0 sugar in either tea or mocha.

Answers on page 173.

Girls' Names Letter Box

LOGIC   **PLANNING**

The letters in the name ZOE can be found in boxes 4, 17, and 19, but not necessarily in that order. The same is true for the other girls' names indicated. Insert all the letters of the alphabet into the boxes. If you do this correctly, the shaded cells will reveal another name.

Hint: Look for words that share a single letter. For example, KATE shares an **A** with LAURA and an **E** with QUEENIE. By comparing the number lists, you can then deduce the value of these letters.

1	2	3	4	5	6	7	8	9	10	11	12	13

14	15	16	17	18	19	20	21	22	23	24	25	26

BETH: 5, 7, 17, 25

BRENDA: 5, 15, 17, 18, 20, 23

CILLA: 21, 22, 23, 24

DAVINA: 15, 16, 20, 21, 23

FRANCES: 6, 10, 17, 18, 20, 22, 23

GLADYS: 6, 12, 14, 15, 23, 24

JOSIE: 1, 6, 17, 19, 21

KATE: 3, 17, 23, 25

LAURA: 13, 18, 23, 24

MARY: 14, 18, 23, 26

MAXINE: 2, 17, 20, 21, 23, 26

PATSY: 6, 11, 14, 23, 25

QUEENIE: 8, 13, 17, 20, 21

WANDA: 9, 15, 20, 23

ZOE: 4, 17, 19

Answers on page 173.

Crossword Snack

Enjoy a quick mental workout? This one's for you. Answer the clues to fill the crossword square with just 10 words.

ACROSS

1. Unspoken
6. Express a view
7. Lincoln bills
8. Bat an eye?
9. Religious spin-offs

DOWN

1. Stylish gents, in British slang
2. Make ___ (get rich)
3. Honda model
4. Like neon
5. SATs

Garbage Bag

Ignoring spaces and punctuation, how many occurrences of the consecutive letters B-A-G can you find in the paragraph below?

Gabby bagged scraps of garbage in a plastic bag and dragged them to the curb aggressively, hoping to grab a glimpse of the cute garbage man, Bob, a guy with a lot of baggage who played bagpipes and was a rumba guru. At the curb, a gust of wind knocked Gabby over and gave her lumbago. Gabby knew she'd never dance the rumba again but hoped to make Bob agog with her homemade baguettes. Bob, aghast at the sight of Gabby on the curb, agreed to dinner after grabbing her arm and bringing her back to the garbage truck.

Answers on page 173.

Jigshape

Can you visually fit the 4 pieces together to form a rounded square?

Wacky Wordy

CREATIVE
THINKING   LANGUAGE

Can you "read" the phrase below?

SHGETAPE

Answers on page 173.

Crossword Snack

Enjoy a quick mental workout? This one's for you. Answer the clues to fill the crossword square with just 10 words.

ACROSS

1. Work hard from the ___ (start)
6. Get the jump on
7. Knock one's top off?
8. "Superman" actor Christopher

   _____

9. Fear greatly

DOWN

1. Pumpkin, for example
2. Get in touch with one's ___ child
3. Titter
4. Hawaiian punch fruit
5. Chose

1	2	3	4	5
6				
7				
8				
9				

Wacky Wordy

Can you "read" the phrase below?

STRAIANGHT

Answers on page 173.

Honeycomb Maze

PLANNING   SPATIAL REASONING

Can you find your way through this maze?

START

FINISH

Answer on page 174.

38

Friendly Pickup

COMPUTATION LOGIC

Best friends Speedy and Pokey started their own bicycle package-pickup service, catering to the businesses that lined both sides of the street they lived on. With each side of the street having the same number of businesses, they decided the best plan would be for Speedy to pick up on one side and Pokey to pick up on the other. In the excitement of the first day, Pokey got his bike turned around and picked up packages at the first five businesses on Speedy's side of the street. That's when Speedy caught up to him and took over, so Pokey crossed the street and started visiting the businesses on his side. Living up to his name, Speedy finished the pickups on his side and crossed over to help Pokey, making the pickups at the last nine businesses on Pokey's side of the street. How many more pickups did Speedy make compared to Pokey?

Wacky Wordy

CREATIVE THINKING LANGUAGE

Can you "read" the phrase below?

END

END KICK

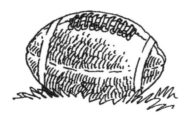

Answers on page 174.

Magazine Rack

Can you make sense of these titles? Below are 6 jumbled phrases or words. Each is an anagram (rearrangement) of a word or phrase that fits the story. Can you decipher all 6?

"Huddle up here, folks," said the journalism instructor to his small group of students at the large downtown newsstand. "These are magazines some of you could be working at someday. And since you deal with language, we're going to have a little fun and mix up the letters a tad. Take this one, for example," he said, picking up a copy of **YELTSIN.** "Would you want to work for a publication that appears to be named for the first president of the Russian federation?"

"Appearances are deceiving," piped up a female student at his side. "That magazine actually deals with fashion, beauty, and celebrities."

"Very good," said the instructor. "How about this one, called **QUERIES?** An appropriate title for all you question-askers."

"Yeah, but that's an old-timey man's magazine," said a young man in the group. "These days it's outpaced by *Maxim* and *Blender* and all the other 'lad mags.' "

"Aha. How about **ORAL GUM** then, or **TEN-FOUR?** Anyone here want to work for them?"

Another girl chimed in. "**ORAL GUM** would be fun if you had a passion for fashion," she said. "And **TEN-FOUR** is strictly for business types, not CBers on the road."

"Right you are," said the instructor. "Here's one called **RATIFY IVAN.** What's it about?"

"Well," said a student, "it's pretty famous for a 1991 cover of Demi Moore naked and pregnant. And it's known for top photographers and good articles."

"You folks are on target today," the instructor beamed. "Here's your last choice, a magazine I'm calling **ORLON SNIGLET.** Want to work for it?"

"Sure! That magazine rocks!" said a girl whose sweatshirt read "I'm with the band."

Answers on page 174.

Missing Connections

It's a crossword without the clues! Use the letters below to fill in the empty spaces in the crossword grid. When you are finished, you'll have words that read both across and down, crossword-style.

A C E E E F H H I I I K L N
O O O O Q R R R T T T T U Y Y Y

Wacky Wordy

Can you "read" the phrase below?

CHIMADENA

Answers on page 174.

Lost in the Pentagon

You need to get to the center of the pentagon to give top secret information to the chief and then dash out the back way. Can you find your way?

Answer on page 174.

Remember Me? (Part 1)

Look at the objects below for 2 minutes, then turn the page and see how many of the objects you remember.

Remember Me? (Part II)

Put a check in the squares of the words that you saw on the preceding page.

- ☐ Slipper
- ☐ Paintbrush
- ☐ Flames
- ☐ Gargoyle
- ☐ Hula Hoop

- ☐ Tent
- ☐ Hot Dog
- ☐ Balloons
- ☐ Goat
- ☐ Acorns

- ☐ Headset
- ☐ Scarecrow
- ☐ Decoys

Math Grid

COMPUTATION   LOGIC

Fill each square in the grid with a digit from 1 through 9. When the numbers in each row are added, you should arrive at the total in the right-hand column. When the numbers in each column are added, you should arrive at the total on the bottom line. The numbers in each diagonal must add up to the totals in the upper and lower right corners.

```
                15
      | 2 | 6 | 1 |   16
  | 1 | 3 | 4 |       10
  | 3 |   | 2 | 5 |   12
      | 3 |   | 4 |   16
  19  10  13  12   16
```

Answers on page 174.

Acrostic Anagram

Unscramble the words below, then transfer the corresponding letters to the grid.
When you're finished, you'll be rewarded with a quote from Will Rogers.

1 K	2 G	3 H	■	4 B	5 A	6 J	7 K	■	8 F	9 A	10 A	■	11 D	12 E	13 I	14 C	■	15 B	16 E
17 L	18 L	19 J	20 H	21 G	22 C	23 H	24 H	25 K	26 F	■	27 I	28 G	29 A	30 B	■	31 E	32 L	33 I	34 F
35 F	36 E	37 G	■	38 J	39 D	40 B	■	41 L	42 E	■	43 C	44 L	45 I	46 D	47 H	■	48 C	49 J	50 C
■	51 H	52 I	53 I	54 F	■	55 J	56 B	57 K	58 H	■	59 C	60 F	61 K	■	62 K	■	63 G	64 D	65 D
■	66 A	67 B	68 A																

A. 9 29 68 66 5 10

_ _ _ _ _ _
Y A Y N W A

B. 67 40 4 30 56 15

_ _ _ _ _ _
T C R I A C

C. 48 22 14 43 50 59

_ _ _ _ _ _
Y W T E A R

D. 11 39 65 64 46

_ _ W _ _
E W R T O

E. 36 12 31 16 42

_ _ A _ _
I C A N H

F. 34 35 26 60 54 8

_ _ N _ _ _
N Y A N S O

G. 28 21 2 63 37

_ _ _ _ _
Z O E O N

H. 3 23 24 58 20 51 47

_ _ _ _ _ _ _
Y I U T I L T

I. 52 53 13 33 45 27

_ _ _ _ _ _
E D H A E V

J. 38 19 49 6 55

_ _ _ _ _
A N K L F

K. 57 62 1 25 61 7

_ A _ _ _ _
U O A Y T L

L. 44 41 17 18 32

_ _ _ _ _
D I V V I

Answers on page 174.

Figuring Fast Food

Fast Food Frank stopped in a brand new burger joint for his fast food lunch. Checking the lighted menu behind the counter, he saw that the following combinations were available:

Burger and fries: $3.50

Fries and a small drink: $2.25

Small drink and a cookie: $1.50

Burger and cookie: ***

Unfortunately, the lights behind the price of Frank's favorite combo, a burger and cookie, were burned out and he didn't know how much it was. It was the counter clerk's first day on the job, and he didn't know the price either. Luckily, Fast Food Frank was fast at figures and figured out how much a burger and cookie combo costs just by looking at the other combo prices. What is the price of the burger-and-cookie combo?

Trivia on the Brain
Did you know that you have 15 times more neurons in your brain than there are people on this planet?

Answer on page 174.

Boingo Wrapo

Only 1 of the cubes matches the center pattern exactly. Which is it?

Answer on page 174.

Hinky Pinky

The clues below lead to a 2-word answer that rhymes, such as Big Pig or Stable Table. The number in parentheses after each clue gives the number of syllables in each word of the answer. As a bonus, how is the theme related to Old MacDonald?

1. Consumes borscht vegetables (1): __ __ __ __   __ __ __ __ __

2. Three-legged stand for an Apple MP3 player (2): __ __ __ __
   __ __ __ __ __ __

3. Putting a stop to mixing coffee beans (2): __ __ __ __ __ __ __
   __ __ __ __ __ __ __

4. Cause bodily harm to Astaire's dance partner Rogers (2): __ __ __ __ __ __
   __ __ __ __ __

5. Comedian's bit about an acorn tree (1): __ __ __   __ __ __ __

Theme:_____

Sudoku

Use deductive logic to complete the grid so that each row, each column, and each 3×3 box contains the numbers 1 through 9 in some order. The solution is unique.

	3	5						4
8			1		9	5		
	6	4			3	1	7	
			9	5				1
				3				
1				7	2			
	5	6	3			9	1	
		9	6		4			5
3				5	2			

Answers on pages 174–175.

On Your Head

Every word listed is contained within the group of letters below. The words can be found in a straight line horizontally, vertically, or diagonally. The words can be read backward or forward.

BEANY (var.)	FELT	PILLBOX
BERET	FEZ	SOMBRERO
BONNET	HELMET	STETSON
CAP	HOMBURG	STRAW
CLOCHE	HOOD	TOPPER
DERBY	KEPI	TURBAN
FEDORA	PANAMA	

```
F  W  A  R  T  S  H  E  L  M  E  T
E  D  R  O  N  O  S  T  E  T  S  X
D  O  Y  G  M  M  T  L  E  F  P  O
O  O  T  B  E  B  E  A  N  Y  A  B
R  H  U  A  R  R  E  Z  W  R  N  L
A  R  R  I  P  E  K  R  E  D  A  L
G  Y  B  N  E  R  D  A  E  F  M  I
L  P  A  C  L  O  C  H  E  T  A  P
B  O  N  N  E  T  R  E  P  P  O  T
```

Answers on page 175.

Venomous

ACROSS

1. Messy eater's protection
4. Diet soda from Coca-Cola
7. Movie western
12. Bruce Springsteen's "Born in the ___"
13. In the manner of
14. Temperature taker
15. PC link, for short
16. Invertebrate with stinging tentacles
18. ___ California
20. GameCube alternative
21. Formation of flying geese
22. Arthropod with a stinging tail
24. "Showgirls" actress Gershon
25. Parks on a bus?
26. Religious pamphlet
27. Madras garments
30. Backless slippers
31. Show without a doubt
32. Check the price of, in a way
34. Provide relief
35. Swimmer with a barbed tail
39. Court grp.
40. Head for the heights
41. Roof projection
42. Longest venomous snake
45. Restriction
46. Actress Roberts
47. Blockhead
48. Small amount
49. Lunch time, for some
50. Jargon suffix
51. In poor health

DOWN

1. Light sources
2. Asimov of science fiction
3. Picked instrument
4. ___ Mahal
5. Joan's role on "Dynasty"
6. Surname of fictional boxer Rocky
7. July birthstone
8. "___ Wiedersehen"
9. Kind of pursuit?
10. Spirit
11. Puts in a microwave, maybe
17. Chaney of horror films
19. Hit the big time
23. Yoga posture
24. Rock genre out of Seattle
26. Secret Service agent, briefly
27. Have a conversation with
28. Regal horse
29. Country singer Cash
32. Not volatile
33. Thin, wispy cloud type
35. Michigan-Ontario canals
36. Hassidic leader
37. Be of use

38. Barbra Streisand film
40. Fraudulent action

43. Swindle
44. Generation

```
 1  2  3  ■  4  5  6  ■  7  8  9  10 11
12        ■ 13       ■ 14
15        ■ 16    ■ 17    ■       21
18     19 ■ 20          ■ 21
22     ■ 23          ■ 24
 ■  ■ 25          ■ 26
27 28 29       ■  ■ 30
31          ■ 32 33    ■  ■  ■
34       ■ 35          36 37 38
39    ■ 40       ■ 41
42    43          44 ■ 45
46          ■ 47       ■ 48
49          ■ 50       ■ 51
```

Trivia on the Brain

Scientists have identified the "oops" center of the human brain. There is a specific region of the brain that reacts when you realize you have made a mistake.

Answers on page 175.

Four-Letter Anagrams

LANGUAGE

Fill in the blanks in each sentence below with 4-letter words that are anagrams (re-arrangements) of one another.

1. The people could not _____ without fear under the rule of the _____ king.

2. Chef _____ needed _____ juice for the recipe.

3. Ted didn't do very _____ without his _____ Artie.

4. The gardener had no _____ for the _____ who ruined his flowers.

5. When the plane _____, the edge of its _____ hit a wire.

6. The speaker _____ many interesting things from the _____.

7. His knees felt _____ when he _____ from his kneeling position.

8. Marissa was excited as she _____ the letter from her _____ friend.

9. The shepherd put some _____ on the sore leg of the _____ .

10. In a year's _____, some factories _____ tons of pollutants into the air.

Math Grid

LOGIC   COMPUTATION

							27
2	3	5		1	7		22
2	3		4	3	6		19
6		8	7		1		39
	2	5		4	2		17
4		3	6		5		27
	2	1	6	3			19
18	21	23	30	26	25	27	

Fill each square in the grid with a digit from 1 through 9. When the numbers in each row are added, you should arrive at the total in the right-hand column. When the numbers in each column are added, you should arrive at the total on the bottom line. The numbers in each diagonal must add up to the totals in the upper and lower right corners.

Answers on page 175.

Black Hole Maze

Can you make your way from the start to the black-hole finish?

FINISH

START

Answer on page 175.

Acrostic Anagram

Unscramble the words below, then transfer the corresponding letters to the grid. When you're finished, you'll be rewarded with a quote from Denis Waitley.

1 A	2 B	3 F	4 H	5 G	6 B	■	7 I	8 E	9 I	■	10 H	11 I	12 A	13 A	14 H	15 B	16 G	17 B	18 C
19 G	■	20 F	21 F	22 E	23 H	24 I	25 A	■	26 B	27 J	28 F	■	29 D	30 I	31 D	32 J	33 A	34 J	35 G
36 I	37 A	38 E	39 I	40 C	■	41 B	42 E	43 F	■	44 H	45 C	46 A	47 B	48 H	49 E	■	50 J	51 H	52 B
53 A	54 D	55 H	56 C	57 C	■	58 F	59 B	60 I	61 D	■	62 B	63 G	64 J	■	65 D	66 H	67 C	68 H	69 D
70 H	71 J	72 C	73 A	74 D	75 G	76 I													

A. 1 37 25 73 46 12 53 33 13
_ _ _ _ _ _ _ _ _
A T R A A N A M C

B. 26 2 15 59 6 41 17 47 52 62
_ _ _ _ _ _ _ _ _ _
R B T E O E U T A H

C. 18 45 67 57 56 40 72
_ _ A _ _ _ _
F T E L E L A

D. 54 65 69 31 29 61 74
_ _ _ _ _ _ _
U B U C M S C

E. 38 49 42 22 8
_ _ _ _ _
E C H B N

F. 58 20 21 3 43 28
_ _ _ _ _ _
D A C E F A

G. 63 16 5 35 75 19
_ _ _ _ _ _
G A E H G L

H. 10 51 66 48 70 44 14 23 4 68 55
_ _ _ _ _ _ _ _ _ _ _
E E V N E N G C R C O

I. 7 36 39 9 24 11 60 30 76
_ _ _ _ _ _ _ _ _
P O N H E E L T E

J. 27 50 71 32 64 34
_ _ _ _ _ _
N Y E H H P

Answers on page 175.

Name Calling

ATTENTION   VISUAL SEARCH

Decipher the encoded word in the quip below using the numbers and letters on the phone pad. Remember that each number can stand for 3 or 4 possible letters.

Never 8–6–3–3–7–3–7–8–4–6–2–8–3 the power of the irate customer.

1	2 ABC	3 DEF
4 GHI	5 JKL	6 MNO
7 PQRS	8 TUV	9 WXYZ
	0	

Can You Find It?

LANGUAGE   ATTENTION   VISUAL SEARCH

Ignoring spaces and punctuation, can you find all 15 occurrences of the consecutive letters F-I-N-D in the paragraph below?

Jeff indicated he found a lot of stuff in Dallas when he left Flint indiscreetly to work as a pathfinder with the deaf Indian he met while searching for some kind of indigo-colored staff in desolate corners of town. A refined fisherman who felt stiff indoors, Jeff fried a fish he caught and had the fin delivered to a friend in Flint, a buff inductee in the Finnish air force named Findley. Finding himself in dire need of funds, Findley sold the fin despite warnings from Jeff indicating it would put his life in disarray.

Answers on page 175.

Jigshape

Can you visually fit the 6 pieces together to form a T?

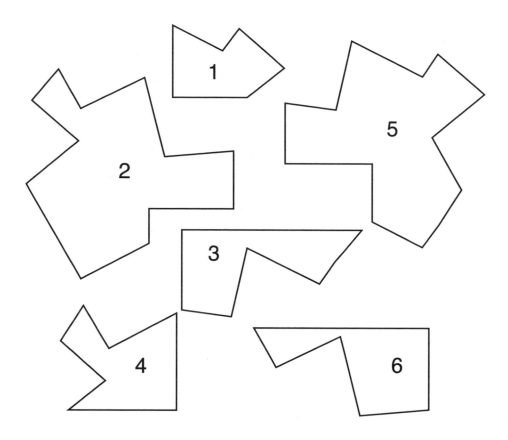

Answer on page 176.

Missing Connections

It's a crossword without the clues! Use the letters below to fill in the empty spaces in the crossword grid. When you are finished, you'll have words that read both across and down, crossword-style.

A D D E F F G H N N N R R R R T T T T U V V

Holiday Anagram

What 2 words, formed from different arrangements of the same 6 letters, can be used to complete the sentence below?

At Christmastime in Bavaria, every _____ village displays a crèche scene with the baby Jesus lying in a _____.

Answers on page 176.

Word Columns

LOGIC   **PLANNING**   **SPATIAL REASONING**

Find the hidden phrase by using the letters directly below each of the blank squares.
Each letter is used only once.

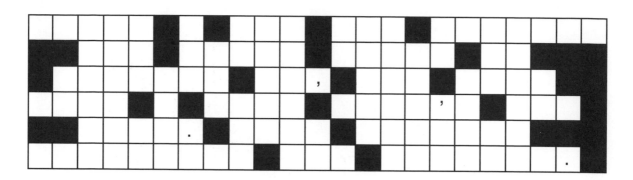

```
  w  a              e        r        s
  g  r  e        n  m  w     h  u  a     s  i  e
  a  u  n  t  n  w  k  o  e  m     e  o  a  l  d  e  r  a  l
O  o  t  h  n  r  s  h  s  o  e     w  b  e  t  u  l  e  n  p
c  o  t  e  i  l  i  t  g  o  t  e  t  s  n  t  f  d  e  r  i  n
d  f  t  n  u  e  l  e  S  l  a  r  t  h  m  e  l  t  e  l  o  t  g
```

What a Racket

ANALYSIS   **CREATIVE THINKING**

Can you determine the missing letter in this progression?

$$G, S, \_\_$$

Answers on page 176.

Screwprint: Criss-Cross

Two identical screws are placed on a sheet of paper as shown. If the top screw is rolled to the right and the bottom screw is rolled up, what pattern will they make?

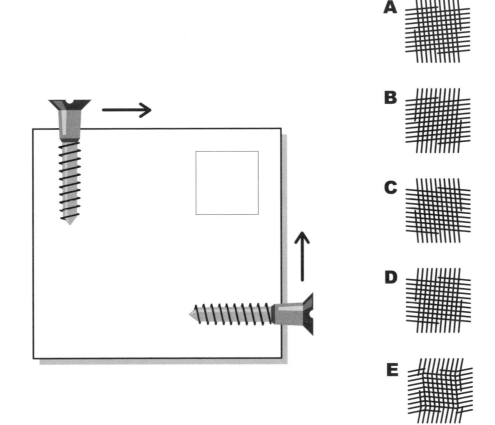

A

B

C

D

E

Answer on page 176.

Sudoku

Use deductive logic to complete the grid so that each row, each column, and each 3×3 box contains the numbers 1 through 9 in some order. The solution is unique.

	1	2	5				3	
					1			
	4				9	5		
7	6	1			3			2
2		4				6		5
9			2			1	7	3
		6	3				8	
			4					
	9				6	3	2	

Trivia on the Brain

It was long believed that emotion and reason were two separate functions of the brain. We now know that emotion is essential to our overall mental health. Why else would physical brain malfunctions cause emotional pain and depression and positive changes effect happiness and laughter?

Answers on page 176.

Crypto-Game Families

Cryptograms are messages in substitution code. Break the code to read the message. For example, THE SMART CAT might become FVO QWGDF JGF if **F** is substituted for **T**, **V** for **H**, **O** for **E**, and so on. The code is different for each crypto-game family.

1. Ball Games	**2. Card Games**	**3. Board Games**
ILKRNDILCC	SJAHBC	POKJJ
HFCF	CDREJC	JPBEIICK
SFCP	FAGIREPC	POKPLKBJ
MAFGJND	RKGKLOK	HFRFMFCA
BFCCNOILCC	BAG JDTTU	IENNCKJOSM
DNTTEK	RJKNU CABEOL	TEHK FU CSUK
PFFDILCC	FIMCJ	POSRKJK POKPLKBJ
IFMMN	ECKJOL	MEBPOKKJS
ILKNILCC	LIPAOKAJC	PCDK
KFMMNA	SKRRKJKO	JFBBA

Answers on page 176.

61

Poker Logic

Ace Grace loved to play poker with her two best friends and their husbands. She's planning her next poker party and wants to avoid duplicating the seating arrangement of the last poker party, which resulted in a big fight over poker chips, potato chips, and chocolate chip cookies. Unfortunately, Ace Grace didn't write the seating arrangement down, but she remembered a few things about where everyone was sitting at the round card table.

Ace Grace did not sit next to her husband.

Wild Winnie sat to the left of the man who sat to the left of the woman who sat to the left of the man who sat to the left of the woman who sat to the left of Ace Grace's husband.

King sat to the left of the woman who sat to the left of Trey.

Jack sat to the left of the woman who sat to the left of the man who sat to the left of Queenie.

What is the name of Ace Grace's husband, and what was the seating order?

Word Ladders

Change just 1 letter on each line to go from the top word to the bottom word. Do not change the order of the letters. You must have a common English word at each step.

1. SWEAT

_____

_____

_____ see-through

_____

STEEP

2. MANOR

_____

_____

_____ someone who likes to keep their wallet tightly shut

_____

WIPER

Answers on page 176.

Mythology Letter Box

The letters in MARS can be found in boxes 3, 4, 6, and 23, but not necessarily in that order. The same is true for the other mythological names indicated. Insert all the letters of the alphabet into the boxes. If you do this correctly, the shaded cells will reveal 2 more names.

Hint: Look for words that share a single letter. For example, AJAX shares an **A** with ACHILLES and a **J** with JUPITER. By comparing the number lists, you can then deduce the values of these letters.

1	2	3	4	5	6	7	8	9	10	11	12	13

14	15	16	17	18	19	20	21	22	23	24	25	26
											W	Q

ACHILLES: 1, 2, 4, 6, 9, 15, 20

AJAX: 4, 10, 19

APHRODITE: 1, 2, 3, 4, 5, 13, 15, 17, 24

APOLLO: 4, 9, 13, 24

BACCHUS: 1, 4, 6, 11, 18, 20

FLORA: 3, 4, 8, 9, 13

GORGONS: 3, 6, 12, 13, 14

HYDRA: 1, 3, 4, 5, 22

JUPITER: 2, 3, 10, 11, 15, 17, 24

MARS: 3, 4, 6, 23

NIKE: 2, 12, 15, 21

VENUS: 2, 6, 11, 12, 16

ZEUS: 2, 6, 7, 11

Answers on page 176.

Sudoku

Use deductive logic to complete the grid so that each row, each column, and each 3×3 box contains the numbers 1 through 9 in some order. The solution is unique.

				3	5		7	
		5	8				6	4
			7		9	2		
		8	3				9	6
			7	8	6			
7	6				9	4		
	1	7		2				
6	8				7	5		
	2		1	6				

Out of the World Anagram

What 2 words, formed from different arrangements of the same 6 letters, can be used to complete the sentence below?

The fiery _____ hurtled through the sky before crashing to earth in a

_____, uninhabited part of Tajikistan.

Answers on page 176.

Acrostic Anagram

Unscramble the words below, then transfer the corresponding letters to the grid. When you're finished, you'll be rewarded with a quote from Agnes Repplier.

1 G	2 D	3 H	4 H	5 D	■	6 D	7 A	8 K	9 A	10 H	11 C	■	12 L	13 D	14 K	15 G	16 I	17 E	18 A
■	19 I	20 J	21 J	■	22 K	23 E	24 K	25 F	26 F	27 B	28 H	29 C	30 A	■	31 F	32 H	33 L	34 L	35 E
■	36 B	37 I	38 H	39 B	40 D	41 G	■	42 J	■	43 B	44 K	45 B	46 C	47 L	48 B	■	49 K	50 E	51 J
■	52 C	53 F	54 A	55 J	■	56 F	57 G	58 J	59 E	60 F	61 A	62 D	63 I	■	64 G	65 H	66 K	67 D	68 L
69 C	70 L	71 C	72 I	73 B	74 J	75 G	76 G												

A. 18 7 30 9 61 54

_ _ _ _ _ _

T N E D S R

B. 36 48 27 39 73 45 43

_ _ _ _ _ _ _

B D D N E R A

C. 29 52 71 69 46 11

_ L _ _ _ _

S L S A C P

D. 6 2 13 40 62 67 5

_ _ _ _ _ _ _

G B N U R E L

E. 17 23 50 59 35

_ _ _ _ _

O E H N Y

F. 26 53 56 31 60 25

_ _ F _ _ _

F I E N R E

G. 57 64 41 1 15 75 76

_ _ _ _ _ _ _

N U G I S H R

H. 3 4 32 28 38 65 10

_ _ _ _ _ _ _

M I N N R O G

I. 19 72 16 37 63

_ _ _ R _

A Y R G N

J. 51 74 55 21 42 58 20

_ _ _ _ _ _ _

N I I A D D S

K. 66 44 22 49 8 24 14

_ E _ _ _ _ _

T S L A I E D

L. 33 68 12 47 34 70

_ _ I _ _ _

I N R E O T

Answers on page 176.

Hinky Pinky

The clues below lead to a 2-word answer that rhymes, such as Big Pig or Stable Table. The number in parentheses after each clue gives the number of syllables in each word in the answer.

1. Lass's ringlets (1): _ _ _ _' _ _ _ _ _ _

2. Big expense on a credit card bill (1): _ _ _ _ _ _ _ _ _ _ _

3. Snapshot of Dorothy's dog in Oz (2): _ _ _ _ _ _ _ _ _

4. Being fond of an ancient Scandinavian raider (2): _ _ _ _ _ _

_ _ _ _ _ _

5. Restricting flaw of a knockoff (4): _ _ _ _ _ _ _ _

_ _ _ _ _ _ _ _ _ _

Name Calling

Decipher the encoded words in the quip below using the numbers and letters on the phone pad. Remember that each number can stand for 3 or 4 possible letters.

The large print 4–4–8–3–8–4, but the small print 8–2–5–3–8–4 away.

1	2 ABC	3 DEF
4 GHI	5 JKL	6 MNO
7 PQRS	8 TUV	9 WXYZ
	0	

Answers on page 177.

Things You Shouldn't Touch (Part I)

Look at the crossword for 2 minutes. Time yourself! Then turn the page, and see how many of the 10 words you remember.

Things You Shouldn't Touch (Part II)

Check off the words you saw in the crossword on page 67.

- ☐ POISON IVY
- ☐ COPPERHEADS
- ☐ PEPE LE PEW
- ☐ POISON-DART FROGS
- ☐ TOXIC PASTE
- ☐ ROADKILL
- ☐ PAINTED FOOD
- ☐ TAINTED WOOD
- ☐ OLEANDER
- ☐ NEW AGE
- ☐ TAINTED FOOD
- ☐ RATTLESNAKES

It's a Gas!

LANGUAGE **CREATIVE THINKING**

Can you figure out what type of gas this is?

$$H_5L_9U_{13}$$

Answers on page 177.

Math Grid

LOGIC COMPUTATION

Fill each square in the grid with a digit from 1 through 9. When the numbers in each row are multiplied, you should arrive at the total in the right-hand column. When the numbers in each column are multiplied, you should arrive at the total on the bottom line. The numbers in each diagonal must multiply to the totals in the upper and lower right corners.

				108
4	5	5		300
2	6		4	144
1			2	30
	2	6		192
32	180	450	96	480

Name Calling

ATTENTION   VISUAL SEARCH

Decipher the encoded word in the quip below using the numbers and letters on the phone pad. Remember that each number can stand for 3 or 4 possible letters.

4–6–2–4–4–6–2–8–4–6–6 is the highest kite that one can fly.

1	2 ABC	3 DEF
4 GHI	5 JKL	6 MNO
7 PQRS	8 TUV	9 WXYZ
	0	

Answers on page 177.

Feeding Time

Mrs. Many has quadruplets with different food preferences. She usually feeds them in a certain order but has managed to mix up all the details in her diary. Although each name, food, and amount is in the correct column, only 1 item in each column is correctly positioned. Using the clues below, can you put the names, food preferences, and amounts in the proper order?

	Name	Food	Spoonfuls
1	Alice	chicken	15
2	Bill	tuna	10
3	Connie	beef	12
4	Des	rabbit	13

1. The 12 spoonfuls are not fed second.
2. Bill is fed 2 places ahead of the tuna-eater.
3. Alice gets the most food.
4. Either chicken or tuna is served fourth.
5. Either Connie or Des eats just after a baby who gets either 12 or 13 spoonfuls of either chicken or tuna.

Name Calling

1	2 ABC	3 DEF
4 GHI	5 JKL	6 MNO
7 PQRS	8 TUV	9 WXYZ
	0	

Decipher the encoded word in the quip below using the numbers and letters on the phone pad. Remember that each number can stand for 3 or 4 possible letters.

We are all 6–2–6–8–3–2–2–8–8–7–3–7–7: making good, making trouble, or making excuses.

Answers on page 177.

Boys' Names Letter Box

The letters in the name BILL can be found in boxes 2, 8, and 18, but not necessarily in that order. The same is true for the other boys' names indicated. Insert all the letters of the alphabet into the boxes. If you do this correctly, the shaded cells will reveal 2 more names.

Hint: Look for words that share a single letter. For example, PAUL shares a **P** with STEPHEN and an **A** with MAX. By comparing the number lists, you can then deduce the values of these letters.

1	2	3	4	5	6	7	8	9	10	11	12	13

14	15	16	17	18	19	20	21	22	23	24	25	26

BARRY: 6, 7, 18, 24

BILL: 2, 8, 18

CARL: 4, 6, 7, 8

DAVID: 2, 6, 16, 26

FRED: 7, 9, 12, 16

GREGORY: 7, 9, 22, 24, 25

JOHN: 3, 5, 22, 23

JIM: 2, 3, 14

MARK: 6, 7, 14, 19

MAX: 6, 14, 15

PAUL: 1, 6, 8, 11

QUENTIN: 2, 9, 11, 17, 21, 23

ROWAN: 6, 7, 13, 22, 23

STEPHEN: 1, 5, 9, 10, 21, 23

ZAK: 6, 19, 20

Answers on page 177.

Aphorism Code-doku

Solve this puzzle just as you do a sudoku. Use deductive logic to complete the grid so that each row, each column, and each 3×3 box contains 1 of the letters of the anagram FISH CRATE. The solution is unique. When you have completed the puzzle, the shaded squares will form a hidden message read top to bottom, from left to right.

C		R			S			
A		H			C		T	
I			E			H		
H	S		I		A			
			H		R		F	
			E	S				
	F		C	T		H		
					S			
	C			R		E		

Hidden message:_____

Marital Anagram

What 2 words, formed from different arrangements of the same 7 letters, can be used to complete the sentence below?

At the double wedding, the two _____ of honor entered the church by passing underneath the rectangular, stained-glass _____ window built above the twin doors.

Answers on page 177.

Red, White, and Blue

Each row, column, and long diagonal contains 2 reds, 2 whites, and 2 blues. From the clues given, can you complete the grid?

Hint: Start at clue B, and don't forget that there are 2 of each color in the long diagonals.

1. Each blue is directly right of each white.
2. Both the reds are directly enclosed by both the blues.
3. No clue needed.
4. The pattern of colors takes the form abcabc.
5. The whites are separated by 3 cells.
6. No clue needed.

A. A blue is directly enclosed by the 2 whites.
B. A white is enclosed by 2 reds, the other by 2 blues.
C. No clue needed.
D. The whites are between the reds.
E. The reds are between the whites.
F. The blues are adjacent.

	A	B	C	D	E	F
1						
2						
3						
4						
5						
6						

Answers on page 177.

Math Grid

Fill each square in the grid with a digit from 1 through 9. When the numbers in each row are multiplied, you should arrive at the total in the right-hand column. When the numbers in each column are multiplied, you should arrive at the total on the bottom line. The numbers in each diagonal must multiply to the totals in the upper and lower right corners.

			30
	1	3	18
4	5		120
		4	48
48	30	72	120

Word Ladders

Change just 1 letter on each line to go from the top word to the bottom word. Do not change the order of the letters. You must have a common English word at each step.

1. IOTA

_____ roster

_____

_____ the speed at which something occurs

_____

_____ ashen

_____

BALL

2. MEET

_____

_____ be in front of

_____

_____ it'll eat almost anything

_____

TOAD

Answers on page 177.

Crossword Snack

Enjoy a quick mental workout? This one's for you. Answer the clues to fill the cross-word square with just 10 words.

ACROSS

1. School mark
6. Was sweet on
7. In the middle of
8. Pay increase
9. Finished

DOWN

1. Angry stare
2. Caesar, for one
3. Stay away from
4. Thick as a brick
5. Trimmed, as a lawn border

1	2	3	4	5
6				
7				
8				
9				

Barefoot Logic

Barefoot Bob never wears socks, but he knows he has some in his sock drawer. The last time he looked at the socks in the drawer, he saw that all but four were white, all but four were black, and all but four were brown. What's the total number of socks that Barefoot Bob has in his drawer, and how many of each color does he have?

Answers on page 177.

Seeing Double LANGUAGE ATTENTION VISUAL SEARCH

The grid contains 21 phrases in which the letter that ends one of the words is the same letter that begins the next word. These doubled letters are given in the clues below. Use these clues to build the phrase list. Blanks indicate the number of letters in each word.

After you've gotten as many answers as you can in your first run-through of the clues, go to the grid and circle those hidden answer words. Other words and doubled letters that you spot in the grid will help you to answer clues you haven't figured out yet. Grid words will run either horizontally, vertically, or diagonally but always in a straight line.

The uncircled letters in the grid are a hidden message about an odd occurrence at a football event. This sentence contains 4 more phrases with doubled letters.

CLUES

1. Words to a misbehaving canine __ __ D D __ __
2. Musical staff symbol C C __ __ __
3. Capeesh? __ __ __ __ __ U U __ __ __ __ __ __ __ __ __ __?
4. Not kidding __ __ R R __ __ __
5. Prankish present __ __ G G __ __ __
6. Date __ O O __ __
7. Miscellaneous collection __ __ __ B B __ __
8. Get tired __ __ __ W W __ __ __ __
9. Sports museum __ __ __ __ __ __ F F __ __ __
10. Elevated wishes __ __ __ H H __ __ __ __
11. "You have to!" I I __ __ __ __ __
12. Knows for certain __ S S __ __ __
13. An army may impose it __ __ __ __ __ __ __ L L __ __
14. Area of geopolitical turmoil __ __ __ __ __ __ E E __ __ __ __
15. I, V or X, e.g. __ __ __ __ __ N N __ __ __ __ __ __
16. California wind or city __ __ __ __ __ A A __ __
17. Agree to a marriage proposal __ __ Y Y __ __

76

18. Wait patiently   _ _ T   T _ _ _ _ _

19. No-fat dairy product   _ _ _ M   M _ _ _

20. Sirloin-slicing utensil   _ _ _ _ _ K   K _ _ _ _ _

21. Check-negating order   _ _ _ P   P _ _ _ _ _ _ _

Hidden message:_____

```
I N T D E I G R A B B A G
H E B O M S I O G T G T A
S S M Y A S E M S F S A Q
A E U O F U A A I I C K K
Y P I U F R E N S G C K S
Y O B U O E H N T G Y I T
E H A N L F I U F A R T O
S H D D L I A M O G A D P
K G D E A N R E R U E N P
I I O R H K C R R M W M A
M H G S A K C A E J W G Y
M A R T I A L L A W O O M
I R O A N E E T L O R H E
L E G N O T F A U L G L N
K I N D E S I T T I G H T
```

Answers on page 178.

ALL ENGINES WORKING

World Cities Letter Box

LOGIC   PLANNING

The letters in LONDON can be found in boxes 3, 10, 16, and 26, but not necessarily in that order. The same is true for the other cities indicated. Insert all the letters of the alphabet into the boxes. If you do this correctly, the shaded cells will reveal another city.

Hint: Look for words that share a single letter. For example, ROME shares an **O** with SOFIA and an **E** with QUEBEC. By comparing the number lists, you can then deduce the values of these letters.

1	2	3	4	5	6	7	8	9	10	11	12	13

14	15	16	17	18	19	20	21	22	23	24	25	26

BRUSSELS: 7, 9, 18, 19, 21, 26

COPENHAGEN: 1, 3, 4, 5, 6, 16, 18, 24

HELSINKI: 1, 8, 9, 13, 16, 18, 26

JAKARTA: 2, 6, 7, 13, 20

LONDON: 3, 10, 16, 26

MEXICO CITY: 3, 4, 8, 15, 18, 20, 22, 23

QUEBEC: 4, 14, 18, 19, 21

QUEZON CITY: 3, 4, 8, 14, 15, 16, 17, 18, 19, 20

REYKJAVIK: 2, 6, 7, 8, 11, 13, 15, 18

ROME: 3, 7, 18, 23

SANTIAGO: 3, 6, 8, 9, 16, 20, 24

SOFIA: 3, 6, 8, 9, 12

VILNIUS: 8, 9, 11, 16, 19, 26

WARSAW: 6, 7, 9, 25

Answers on page 178.

Cube Crazy

PLANNING SPATIAL REASONING

Three of the 4 shapes below can be formed from cutting Figure 1 into 2 pieces and reassembling it. Which is the odd figure out?

Fig. 1

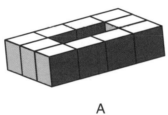

A

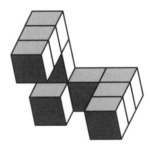

B

C

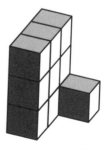

D

Answer on page 178.

Read Between the Lines

You get double the fun with this puzzle—it's a word search, but first you must figure out what words to search for. The words below all contain the consecutive letters L-I-N-E. The number of spaces lets you know how many letters are in the words, and the answers are in alphabetical order. Then find the words in the grid on the next page, but the word LINE has been replaced with a hyphen (-) in the grid. After you've found all the words in the grid, the leftover letters contain a hidden message by an art critic who doesn't consider everything art.

Clues

1. JetBlue competitor _ _ _ _ _ _ _ _ _ _ _ _ _ LINE _
2. Thin and curved, like an eagle's nose _ _ _ _ LINE
3. Marking on a ball field _ _ _ _ LINE
4. Most direct route _ _ _ LINE
5. Dangerous place to be in battle _ _ _ _ _ _ _ _ _ _ _ _ LINE _
6. Waxed body area _ _ _ _ _ _ LINE
7. Dirt-free aim _ _ _ _ _ LINE _ _
8. Reporter's due date _ _ _ _ LINE
9. Rigorous self-control _ _ _ _ _ _ LINE
10. Place to sign on _ _ _ _ _ _ LINE
11. Makeup item _ _ _ LINE _
12. Having a mink-hair inner layer _ _ _ -LINE _
13. Car fuel _ _ _ _ LINE
14. Skirt's bottom edge _ _ _ LINE
15. Cold War phone _ _ _ LINE
16. Rollerblades activity _ _ -LINE _ _ _ _ _ _
17. Johnny Cash classic "_ _ _ _ _ _ _ _ _ LINE"
18. Muttonchops' place _ _ _ LINE
19. Noncellular phone _ _ _ _ LINE
20. "Electric Slide," for one LINE _ _ _ _ _
21. Maximum amount for borrowing LINE _ _ _ _ _ _ _ _
22. Ancestry LINE _ _ _
23. Math branch LINE _ _ _ _ _ _ _ _ _

80

24. Defensive football player L I N E _ _ _ _ _ _

25. Storage area for bedding and towels L I N E _ _ _ _ _ _ _

26. Referring to men _ _ _ _ _ L I N E

27. Hat seller _ _ _ L I N E _

28. It may be plunging _ _ _ _ L I N E

29. Cruise ship _ _ _ _ _ _ L I N E _

30. "I Fall to Pieces" singer _ _ _ _ _ _ _ L I N E

31. Strikers' formation _ _ _ _ _ _ _ L I N E

32. "Come here often?," for one _ _ _ _ _ _ _ L I N E

33. Joke's ending _ _ _ _ _ _ L I N E

34. Lounge chair _ _ _ L I N E _

35. This grid's shape _ _ _ L I N E

36. Opening roster _ _ _ _ _ _ _ _ _ L I N E _ _

37. Sign at a queue _ _ _ L I N E _ _ _ _ _ _ _ _ _ _

38. Chronology _ _ _ _ L I N E

39. Apparatus for bouncing _ _ _ _ _ _ L I N E

40. Beauty's opposite _ _ L I N E _ _

Hidden message:_____

```
                              T
                              H
                              E
                              -
                          A   F   -
                      G   H   O   T   -
                  E   I   S   R   D   -   I
                  R   A   P   M   A   P   N
                  G   M   A   S   C   U   -
                  W   E   T   H   -   K   S                   T   H
                  P   R   S   E   O   C   K           S   K   Y   -
      -   D   A   E   D   U   I   Y   R   F   I   A       E   -   K   A
      W   O   H   -   -   N   C   C   E   C   P   T       R   E   C   -   R   U
      S   T   E   I   E   C   A   -   K   R   N   I   I   -   E   S   A   B   G   T
      S   T   C   N   H   H   N   Q   -   E   O   N   -   N   O   B   E   E   -   F
      -   E   M   I   T   -   A   L   U   D   T   G   B   C   -   P   M   G   S   U
      N   D   R   K   K   D   I   S   C   I   P   -   A   L   M   E   M   L   S   R
      A   -   -   I   L   M   R   J   S   T   -   T   C   O   E   C   N   A   D   -
      E   O   E   B   A   R   -   N   A   E   C   O   K   S   H   -   D   R   R   D
      L   R   Y   A   W   W   S   I   N   W   G   S   E   E   -   D   N   A   L   T
      C   B   E   H   I   N   D   E   N   E   M   Y   -   S   T   A   R   T   I   N   G   -   U   P
```

Answers on page 178.

Sudoku

Use deductive logic to complete the grid so that each row, each column, and each 3×3 box contains the numbers 1 through 9 in some order. The solution is unique.

1				2	9			
		7			8	9		
		3		7				
	9	6	8	1				
	4		9		2		7	
				3	6	2	8	
				9		1		
		1	7			4		
			2	4				7

Ohio Anagram

Fill in the blanks in the sentence below with words that are anagrams (rearrangements) of one another.

The joyriders _____ around _____, Ohio,

and watched as stores were _____ during the riot.

Answers on page 178.

Crypto-Wisdom

Cryptograms are messages in substitution code. Break the code to read the message. For example, THE SMART CAT might become FVO QWGDF JGF if **F** is substituted for **T**, **V** for **H**, **O** for **E**, and so on. The code is different for each cryptogram.

1. FJCCM BL H DBLGLK JA OEK BDHNBIHOBJI.

2. HCB GDKIH HCLJM FEDAH PLIHFNBI LJ HCB

   NLHOCBJ LI HCFH RDA AIAFSSR CFTB HD BFH

   HCBP.

3. HBG'A IBDCLA AEFA FJJDLKMFAMBG MN

   FROFPN FJJDLKMFALH.

Math Grid

Fill each square in the grid with a digit from 1 through 9. When the numbers in each row are added, you should arrive at the total in the right-hand column. When the numbers in each column are added, you should arrive at the total on the bottom line. The numbers in each diagonal must add up to the totals in the upper and lower right corners.

								34
	6	5	8			1	2	34
8	6		9	2	8			40
7		8	5	4			5	35
9		6		9	2	3		44
7	1		4	2	5			31
	2	4	6			4	7	31
5	2	3		6			1	28
42	27	35	43	37	31	28	31	

Answers on pages 178–179.

Star Power

Fill in each of the empty squares in the grid so that each star is surrounded by the numbers 1 through 8 with no repeats.

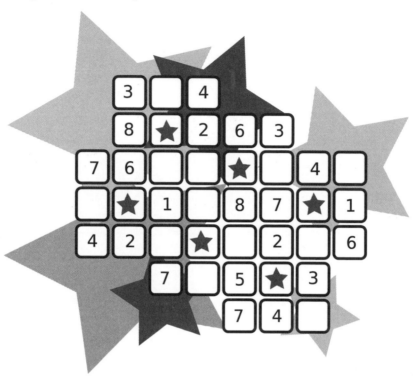

Medical Anagram

Fill in the blanks in the sentence below with words that are anagrams (rearrangements) of one another.

The doctor prescribed a _____ to settle down any strange, high-strung patient

who _____ from the proscribed rules of behavior.

Answers on page 179.

Word Columns

Find the hidden quote and its author by using the letters directly below each of the blank squares. Each letter is used only once.

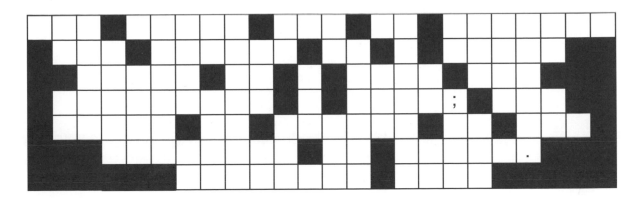

```
                    t               D
            a h a b       e     a         i
          h p s c r s o y y a o r     s     c t m n
        f w e m o n t l v m d p r t o e i o u s g
        o i r f s u e t l r a a f o t t y w t w e
        h b v i t S s e k a e n p o e d i o t h a s
      T t e o o i s i l o s a o n a i a l o a p a r e
```

Trivia on the Brain

In most adults, the language center of the brain is in the left hemisphere. But babies up to a year old respond to language with their entire brains, allowing them to acquire language skills at an impressive rate.

Answers on page 179.

Day at the Zoo

Can you spot the 24 differences between these 2 pictures?

Answers on page 179.

Hinky Pinky

The clues below lead to a 2-word answer that rhymes, such as Big Pig or Stable Table. The number in parentheses after each clue gives the number of syllables in each word in the answer.

1. More out-of-focus mink-coat dealer (3): __ __ __ __ __ __ __ __
__ __ __ __ __ __

2. Lowering of the amount of the penalty for a gymnast's error (3):
__ __ __ __ __ __ __ __ __ __ __ __ __ __ __ __

3. Seriousness of a hole in a tooth (3): __ __ __ __ __ __
__ __ __ __ __ __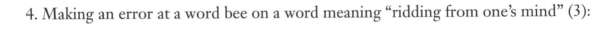

4. Making an error at a word bee on a word meaning "ridding from one's mind" (3):
__ __ __ __ __ __ __ __ __ __ __
__ __ __ __ __ __ __ __ __

5. White radioactive element in a football arena (3): __ __ __ __ __ __ __
__ __ __ __ __ __

Cast-a-Word

There are 4 dice, the faces of which have different letters of the alphabet. (Each letter appears only once.) Random throws of the dice produced the words in this list. Can you figure out which letters appear on each of the 4 dice?

BYRE	GRAY	PAWN	TUCK
CURE	HULK	PLAN	VERY
EXIT	LACE	SHOP	YARD
FAIR	MANE	SLID	ZEAL

Answers on page 179.

Word Jigsaw

Fit the pieces into the frame to form common, uncapitalized words reading across and down crossword-style. There's no need to rotate the pieces; they'll fit as shown, with each piece used exactly once.

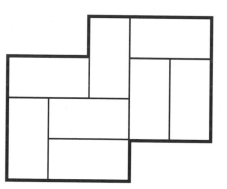

Wacky Wordy

Can you "read" the phrase below?

DGOEE

Answers on page 179.

Missing Connections

It's a crossword without the clues! Use the letters below to fill in the empty spaces in the crossword grid. When you are finished, you'll have words that read both across and down, crossword-style.

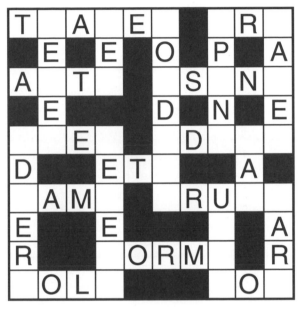

AAABCDDEEEGGHHI
LNNPPRRSTTTUVVW

Wacky Wordy

Can you "read" the phrase below?

TTTTACRES+MULE

Answers on page 179.

Ball Games

ACROSS

1. Designate
4. Oil-burning light
8. It keeps the oxen together
12. Last word of the Pledge of Allegiance
13. One of the Muses
14. Winged Greek god
15. Ancestor of baseball
17. Air ball, e.g.
18. Marquette's title
19. "It's becoming clear"
21. Olympic sport since 1988
27. Diving bird
28. Heart med.
29. Lobbying grps.
32. Network connections
34. The wild blue yonder
35. Gasoline brand
37. Waffle topper
39. Game in which the target is called a jack
42. Lacking quality
43. Rainforest tree
46. Kind of camp
48. Canada's national summer sport
52. Leia's twin brother
53. Rubber stamp
54. "Don't open ___ Xmas"
55. Even scores
56. Passenger list entry
57. Sugary liquid

DOWN

1. Protective ground covering
2. Lotion additive
3. Speak suddenly
4. Type of TV screen
5. Alcoholic beverage
6. Former space station
7. Assume as a given
8. Mocha citizen
9. Points in the right direction
10. Puts on the canvas: abbr.
11. Double twist
16. Talk radio host Boortz
20. Martial arts instructor
22. Pygmy chimpanzee
23. London facility
24. Provide financial support for
25. Drive to distraction
26. Protein source
29. Crony
30. Physicians for Responsible Negotiations org.
31. Ranch hand
33. House alternation
36. $100 bills
38. Not taken in by
40. Acrylic material

41. Tales of adventure
44. Where many Indians live
45. Form of seaweed
46. Club alternative, briefly
47. Nice affirmative
49. Sometimes called: abbr.
50. Motion transformer
51. Sandwich bread choice

1	2	3		4	5	6	7		8	9	10	11
12				13					14			
15			16						17			
18						19	20					
		21		22	23	24					25	26
			27					28				
29	30	31		32		33			34			
35			36			37		38				
39				40					41			
		42						43		44	45	
46	47			48	49	50	51					
52				53					54			
55				56					57			

Trivia on the Brain
The brain needs ten times more oxygen than the rest of the body.

Answers on page 179.

Star Trek Maze

PLANNING   SPATIAL REASONING

Can you find your way to the star at the center of the maze?

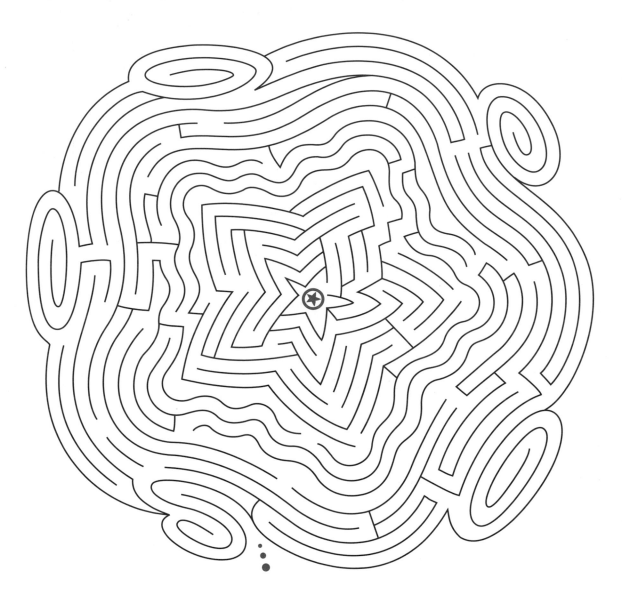

Answer on page 180.

Math Grid

Fill each square in the grid with a digit from 1 through 9. When the numbers in each row are added, you should arrive at the total in the right-hand column. When the numbers in each column are added, you should arrive at the total on the bottom line. The numbers in each diagonal must add up to the totals in the upper and lower right corners.

							27
7	4	5	1	2	9		30
	8	5	4	3		1	30
2		5	9		7	7	40
6	5	4		7	5	6	41
9	8		7	1	4		37
2	1	8		2		4	25
	6		5	3	5	3	31

32 38 36 38 22 40 28 36

Wacky Wordy

Can you "read" the phrase below?

TEAMTEAMCOVERAGE

Answers on page 180.

Acrostic Anagram

Unscramble the words below, then transfer the corresponding letters to the grid. When you're finished, you'll be rewarded with a quote from James Thomson.

1 B	2 F	3 C	4 I	■	5 F	6 E	7 A	8 B	■	9 E	10 G	11 I	■	12 A	13 H	14 B	15 G	■	16 A
17 G	18 E	■	19 H	20 A	21 F	22 I	■	23 C	24 D	■	25 H	26 B	27 E	28 B	29 E	30 C	31 A	■	32 E
33 F	34 D	35 I	36 H	37 B	38 A	■	39 I	40 A	41 B	42 E	■	43 F	44 D	■	45 D	46 A	47 B	48 D	49 C
■	50 B	51 B	52 C	■	53 I	54 F	55 E	56 G	57 E	58 C	59 G	60 A	■	61 A	62 H	63 C	■	64 I	65 D
■	66 F	67 E	68 G	69 B	70 D	71 C	72 H												

A. 46 7 31 20 16 40 60 61 38 12

— — — — — — — — — —

TSSARELEBH

B. 50 51 41 28 1 26 8 47 69 37 14

— — — — — — — — — — —

EOEMRERMTHT

C. 58 71 3 52 30 23 63 49

— — — — — — — —

EOEROGSF

D. 24 45 34 44 70 65 48

— — — — — — —

OYFIRFT

E. 18 27 55 57 29 42 9 32 6 67

— — — — — — — — — —

SIANHAUTEA

F. 5 54 66 33 43 2 21

— — — — — — —

CIFAOTN

G. 15 68 10 59 56 17

— — — — — —

HUUCEN

H. 25 19 13 72 36 62

— — — — — —

NUKHCY

I. 53 35 11 64 39 4 22

— — — — — — —

OIDEDWW

Answers on page 180.

Hinky Pinky

The clues below lead to a 2-word answer that rhymes, such as Big Pig or Stable Table. The number in parentheses after each clue give the number of syllables in each word in the answer.

1. Heap in a pathway inside a plane (1): __ __ __ __ __   __ __ __ __

2. Disconnected reading material for an editor to smooth out (2):

__ __ __ __ __ __   __ __ __ __

3. Yarn about an escargot (1): __ __ __ __ __ __   __ __ __ __

4. Successful oil wells of one who seats people in pews (2): __ __ __ __ __' __

__ __ __ __ __ __

5. Beach footwear of defacers of public property (2): __ __ __ __ __ __ __'

__ __ __ __ __ __ __

Witty Anagram

Fill in the blanks in the sentence below with words that are anagrams (rearrangements) of one another.

Although it might seem like an unusual source of joy, writing witty _____

for tombstones was what made Morticia the _____ woman alive.

Answers on page 180.

Hurry!

ACROSS

1. Wild guess
5. Mont Blanc, e.g.
8. Did in
12. Columbus' home
13. Civil War general
14. Scruff
15. "Hurry!"
17. Like
18. One for the books?
19. Facet
21. Frittata
23. Circumspect
27. Small Pacific salmons
31. Aptly named fruit
32. Slow-witted
34. Presidential caucus state
35. Dark meat choice
37. Bread crumbs, perhaps
39. Not slow paced
41. Small bar
44. Kind of report
49. First place?
50. "Hurry!"
52. Matador's opponent
53. Sensitive subject, to some
54. Writer Ferber
55. Side order

56. Heir, perhaps
57. 49-Across inhabitant

DOWN

1. Counter order
2. Friends' pronoun
3. Isn't incorrect?
4. Two out of two
5. Worried, and then some
6. Maui memento
7. Corolla part
8. "Hurry!"
9. Superior, e.g.
10. Like a DeMille production
11. Left
16. Club choice
20. Dry, as champagne
22. Ruler's decree
23. Kind of instinct
24. "That's disgusting"
25. Baba of "Arabian Nights"
26. "Hurry!"
28. ___ polloi
29. Fess (up)
30. Droop
33. Wet a little
36. Part of H.M.S.
38. Book written by Luke
40. Counter orders

41. Wagers
42. Superstar
43. Immunizing stuff
45. Word with code or rug

46. Mary Lincoln, nee ___
47. Arm bone
48. Bridge coup
51. Pride

Answers on page 180.

Star Power

ATTENTION   COMPUTATION   LOGIC

Fill in each of the empty squares in the grid so that each star is surrounded by the numbers 1 through 8 with no repeats.

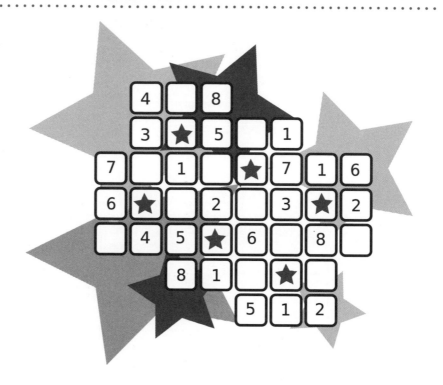

Cat Logic

LOGIC

When Ken the cat walker came down with a case of congestion, he asked his girlfriend Carla to fill in for him. He gave Carla a list of the names of the owners and their cats and warned her not to lose the list because the cats were identical except for the name-tags on their collars. Coincidentally, the cats had the same names as his customers, but no customer owned a cat with his own name.

Carla made the mistake of putting the list in a lunch bag with her tuna sandwich, both of which were eaten when she wasn't looking by a very hungry cat named Stripes. Carla frantically tried to remember which cat belonged to which owner. She was sure that Mr. Puddles did not own Rusty. She knew that the cat owned by Mr. Rusty did not have the same name as the owner of Rusty. She was confident that Mr. Tommy's cat did not have the same name as the man who owned Puddles. She was certain that the cat owned by Mr. Stripes did not have the same name as the owner of Tommy. Help Carla deliver the right cat to the right owner so Ken doesn't lose his customers.

Answers on page 180.

Number Crossword

Fill in this crossword with numbers instead of letters. Use the clues to determine which of the numbers 1 through 9 belongs in each square. No zeros are used.

Hint: Since zeros are not permitted, there are only 4 possibilities for 7-Across. List them.

ACROSS

1. A composite (nonprime) number
3. Consecutive digits, descending
6. Consecutive digits, ascending
7. A multiple of 18

DOWN

1. Nine times 1-Across
2. A composite (nonprime) number
4. Its last digit is the sum of its first 2 digits
5. A perfect square

Math Grid

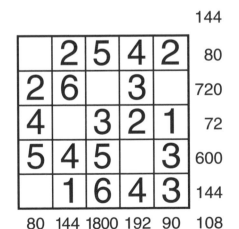

Fill each square in the grid with a digit from 1 through 9. When the numbers in each row are multiplied, you should arrive at the total in the right-hand column. When the numbers in each column are multiplied, you should arrive at the total on the bottom line. The numbers in each diagonal must multiply to the totals in the upper and lower right corners.

Answers on page 180.

Around Three Cubes

Each group of cubes has 1 line that wraps around it. Determine which 2 cubes have lines that make the exact same pattern.

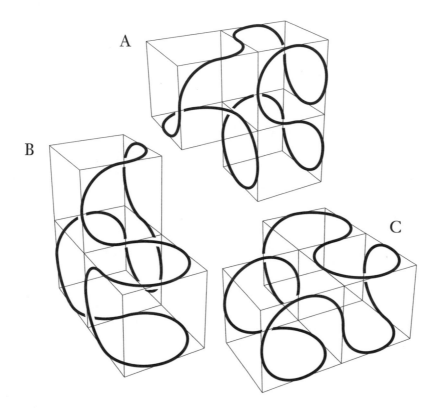

Answer on page 181.

Acrostic Anagram

Unscramble the words below, then transfer the corresponding letters to the grid. When you're finished, you'll be rewarded with a quote from George F. Will.

1 G	2 I		3 D	4 I	5 C	6 B		7 E	8 I	9 G		10 D	11 C		12 D	13 F		14 F	15 G
16 F	17 B	18 D	19 H		20 E	21 I	22 H	23 F	24 F	25 A	26 A	27 E		28 G	29 A	30 E	31 C	32 E
33 I	34 F	35 F	36 C		37 B	38 I	39 B	40 F	41 F	42 B	43 B	44 D	45 F		46 C	47 B	48 E	49 A	50 B
51 F	52 A	53 H	54 H		55 H	56 I		57 H	58 I	59 B	60 G	61 G	62 B	63 B	64 F	65 H		66 H	67 E
	68 A	69 A		70 C	71 E	72 G	73 G												

A. 25 49 69 26 68 29 52
  _ _ _ _ _ _ _
  C A R B E C I

B. 6 59 47 37 62 63 42 43 17 39
  _ _ _ _ _ _ _ _ _ _
  V R T E E I I P E T

C. 70 5 11 36 31 46
  _ _ _ _ _ _
  S E H G U S

D. 18 44 50 10 12 3
  _ _ _ _ _ _
  T E N I T Y

E. 71 30 48 67 7 20 27 32
  _ _ _ _ _ _ _ _
  O R V O Y J S E

F. 64 16 40 23 45 41 35 34 13 24 51 14
  _ _ _ _ _ _ _ _ _ _ _ _
  L O I A G A N A N T I V

G. 15 72 60 1 61 9 28 73
  _ _ _ _ _ _ _ _
  B E I L N V E A

H. 55 54 53 66 19 65 57 22
  _ _ _ _ _ _ _ _
  N E O B G E D L

I. 2 4 58 38 8 33 56 21
  _ _ _ _ _ _ _ _
  L W E L O R F O

Answers on page 181.

Sudoku

Use deductive logic to complete the grid so that each row, each column, and each 3×3 box contains the numbers 1 through 9 in some order. The solution is unique.

					1			2
4	1	5	2					
				7		6		
8				1		4		
	2			4			6	
		7		5				9
		6		8				
					5	7	1	8
9			1					

Genius Anagram

Fill in the blanks in the sentence below with words that are anagrams (rearrangements) of one another.

Would physicist Albert _____ have developed more groundbreaking

theories had he lived well into his _____?

Answers on page 181.

Word Jigsaw

LANGUAGE   SPATIAL PLANNING

Fit the pieces into the frame to form common, uncapitalized words reading across and down crossword-style. There's no need to rotate the pieces; they'll fit as shown, with each piece used exactly once.

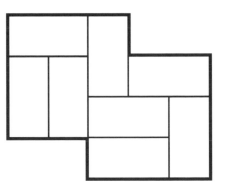

Ageless Logic

LOGIC

Not wanting to be embarrassed by revealing her age on her birthday, Grandma instead told the grandkids that if they multiplied her age in 5 years by 5, then multiplied her age in 6 years by 6, and added the two totals together, they would get a number that is 12 times her current age. When she saw the large wax forest fire atop her birthday cake, Grandma knew they had figured it out. How old is she?

Answers on page 181.

Insect Marriages

Due to a clerical error, the insect marriage office has no idea who they are expecting and in what order. In their log, although each item is in the correct column, only 1 item is correctly positioned in each column.

	Groom	Bride	Surname
1	ant	flea	Kent
2	beetle	grasshopper	Loopy
3	cockroach	honeybee	Mags
4	dragonfly	butterfly	Nomad
5	earthworm	wasp	Ozone

The following facts are true about the correct order.

1. The earthworm is 1 place after the butterfly.
2. The wasp is 1 place before the Nomads.
3. The cockroach is not marrying the butterfly nor is it a Nomad.
4. The Kents are 1 place before the honeybee, who is 2 places after the cockroach.
5. The ant is 2 places before the Ozones.

Can you find the correct groom, bride, and surname for each?

Answers on page 181.

Things That Smell Good (Part 1)

LANGUAGE   MEMORY   ATTENTION

Look at the freeform crossword for 2 minutes. Then turn the page to complete this puzzle.

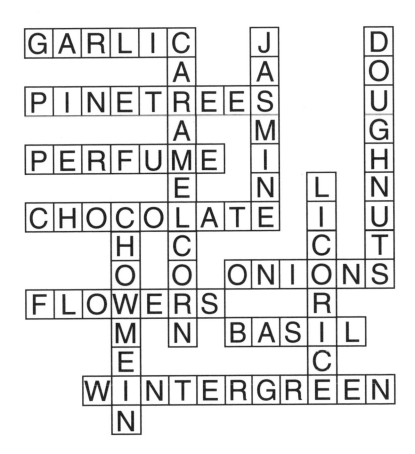

Things That Smell Good (Part II)

Check off the words you saw on the preceding page:

- ☐ GARLIC
- ☐ LILAC
- ☐ JASMINE
- ☐ ONIONS
- ☐ LAVENDER
- ☐ CHOW MEIN
- ☐ LICORICE

- ☐ CARAMEL CORN
- ☐ DAISY
- ☐ FORGET-ME-NOT
- ☐ DOUGHNUTS
- ☐ PERIWINKLE
- ☐ CHOCOLATE

Math Grid

LOGIC **COMPUTATION**

51

6	3	2		2	6	5	33
	2	8	4			9	6	38
4		3	7	5	7			37
2	8	4	8				5	31
7			2	9			8	43
9		5	1	3	2	2	30
	5	6		4	6	3	40

42 39 35 38 28 37 33 33

Fill each square in the grid with a digit from 1 through 9. When the numbers in each row are added, you should arrive at the total in the right-hand column. When the numbers in each column are added, you should arrive at the total on the bottom line. The numbers in each diagonal must add up to the totals in the upper and lower right corners.

Answers on page 181.

Red, White, and Blue

Each row, column, and long diagonal contains 2 reds, 2 whites, and 2 blues. From the clues given, can you complete the grid?

```
    A B C D E F
  1 □ □ □ □ □ □
  2 □ □ □ □ □ □
  3 □ □ □ □ □ □
  4 □ □ □ □ □ □
  5 □ □ □ □ □ □
  6 □ □ □ □ □ □
```

1. Both the whites are directly enclosed by both the reds.
2. The whites are separated by 3 cells.
3. No clue needed.
4. There are no blues or reds in the outer cells.
5. No clue needed.
6. One red is directly enclosed by 2 blues; the other by 2 whites.

A. No clue needed.
B. The reds are adjacent.
C. No clue needed.
D. The pattern of colors is of the form abcabc.
E. No clue needed.
F. The reds are adjacent.

Answers on page 181.

Aphorism Code-doku

Solve this puzzle just as you do a sudoku. Use deductive logic to complete the grid so that each row, each column, and each 3×3 box contains 1 of the letters of the anagram WRONG THEM. The solution is unique. When you have completed the puzzle, the shaded squares will form a hidden message read top to bottom, from left to right.

Hidden message:_____

_____

			M	T			
	O	G					
W							
		O			N	M	R
	G				T		
R					W		
E	H	N			R	O	
	M		H	G			
N			T				

Word Ladders

Change just 1 letter on each line to go from the top word to the bottom word. Do not change the order of the letters. You must have a common English word at each step.

1. PLANT

_____

_____ empty

_____

_____

_____ seawater

BRIDE

2. SANDY

_____

_____ kids love it

_____

DADDY

Answers on page 181.

The Castle of Horror

LANGUAGE | CREATIVE THINKING

Who can be found lurking in this spooky castle? Frankenstein, Wolfman, Boris Karloff, Vincent Price, or Dracula? The castle holds all the clues.

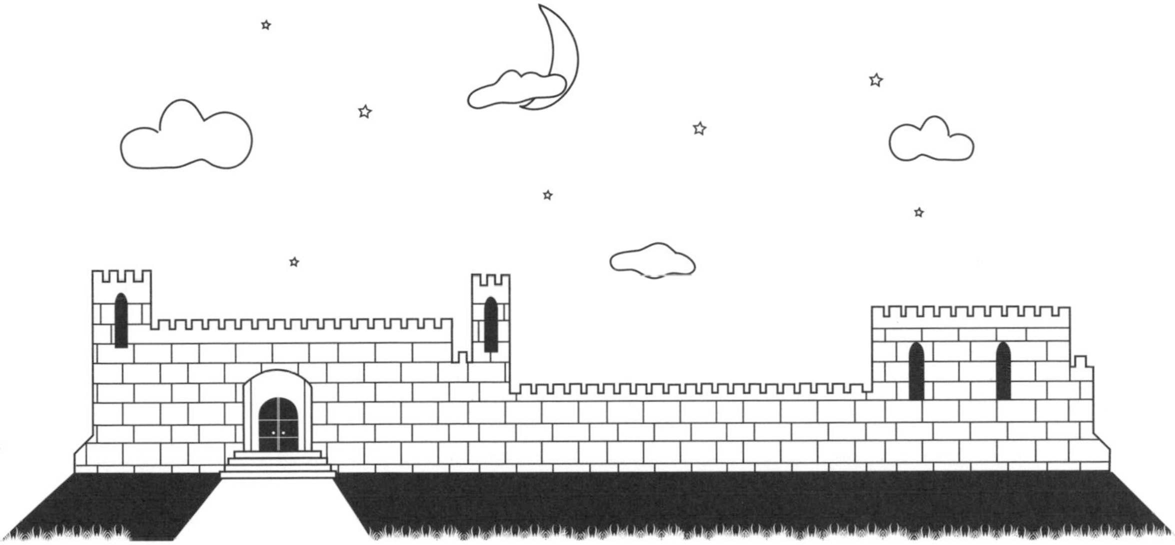

Math Grid

LOGIC | COMPUTATION

					480
5		4	3		360
4	6		5	2	720
3		4		5	720
2	4	6	3		576
	4		3	5	1080
720	1152	864	810	200	1800

Fill each square in the grid with a digit from 1 through 9. When the numbers in each row are multiplied, you should arrive at the total in the right-hand column. When the numbers in each column are multiplied, you should arrive at the total on the bottom line. The numbers in each diagonal must multiply to the totals in the upper and lower right corners.

Answers on pages 181–182.

Word Jigsaw

Fit the pieces into the frame to form common, uncapitalized words reading across and down crossword-style. There's no need to rotate the pieces; they'll fit as shown, with each piece used exactly once.

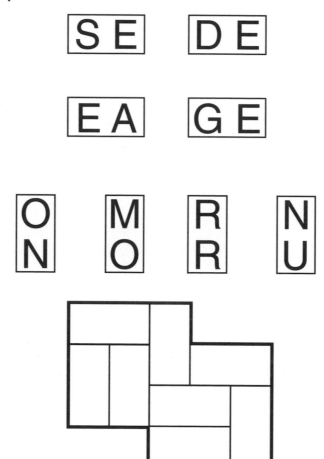

Timely Sequence

Can you determine the missing letter in this progression?

E, C, M, __

Answers on page 182.

Remember Me? (Part I)

Look at the pictures below for 2 minutes. Then turn the page to complete the puzzle.

Remember Me? (Part II)

Check off the items you saw on the preceding page:

- ☐ Cow
- ☐ Easel
- ☐ Calculator
- ☐ Tool belt
- ☐ Molar

- ☐ Football
- ☐ Ponytail
- ☐ Tomahawk
- ☐ Haystack

- ☐ Whale
- ☐ Headset
- ☐ Ears of corn
- ☐ Backpack

Missing Connections

LANGUAGE **PLANNING**

It's a crossword without the clues! Use the letters below to fill in the empty spaces in the crossword grid. When you are finished, you'll have words that read both across and down, crossword-style.

A A A C D D D E F H I L M M
O P R R R S S T T V Y Y Y Z

Answers on page 182.

Word Columns

Find the hidden phrase by using the letters directly below each of the blank squares.
Each letter is used only once.

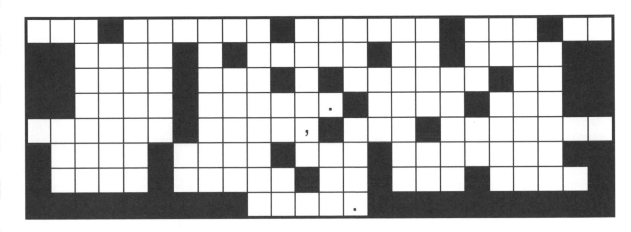

```
                    t
     f    r    u    d              t         a
   k a e      h n a t m    y u    y i u
   o u r r    e e d i a a e    l s d y s n m
 a o o s p    a h s m m n d e o n p y i t r
 o y t e h h e l l t i e w a y c e t o y g n
m y s e c e o a l d y a l t O r h e b t u n t g
Y y u u u r b t a a r a l t r n o b a r o i e o
```

Trivia on the Brain

Scientists have identified the specific region of the brain that causes laughter.

Answers on page 182.

ADDING MORE POWER

Odd-Even Logidoku

LOGIC

Use deductive logic to complete the grid so that each row, column, diagonal, irregular shape, and 3×3 box contains the numbers 1 through 9 in some order. You may only place even numbers in boxes with the letter E. The solution is unique.

Cast-a-Word

LOGIC   PROBLEM SOLVING

There are 4 dice, the faces of which have different letters of the alphabet. (Each letter appears only once.) Random throws of the dice produced the words in this list. Can you figure out which letters appear on each of the 4 dice?

BITE	HELM	NIGH	TILE
BREW	JUMP	POST	TREK
CLAY	JURY	QUIZ	TROD
FLEW	MUTE	RAGE	ZERO

Answers on page 182.

Supermarket Sojourn

This stressed-out mom just wants to go home. Help her find the teddy bear for her daughter, and then find where she placed her purse.

START ▶

▲FINISH

Answer on page 182.

115

Occupation Word Search

LANGUAGE

ATTENTION

VISUAL SEARCH

Every word listed is contained within the group of letters. The words can be found in a straight line horizontally, vertically, or diagonally. The words can be read backward or forward.

ACTOR

BARBER

CARPENTER

DENTIST

ECONOMIST

FARMER

GEOLOGIST

HANDLER

INTERN

JANITOR

KNITTER

LAWYER

MAILMAN

NURSE

ORGANIST

PLUMBER

POET

QUILTER

```
S  I  N  G  E  R  E  T  L  I  U  Q  O
C  R  I  V  E  T  E  R  A  T  R  R  H
T  E  A  E  R  T  S  O  L  S  O  O  Z
S  M  R  T  N  R  E  T  N  I  R  T  M
I  R  M  E  I  L  F  C  T  G  Z  I  R
T  A  Y  R  T  A  W  A  A  O  O  N  T
N  F  N  I  E  T  I  N  N  L  O  A  S
E  C  O  N  O  M  I  S  T  O  L  J  I
D  A  C  A  P  S  E  N  B  E  O  R  G
T  R  L  R  T  X  S  A  K  G  G  E  O
E  P  A  I  R  U  R  X  V  W  I  L  L
A  E  W  A  H  B  U  I  S  T  S  D  O
C  N  Y  N  E  R  N  P  H  O  T  N  R
H  T  E  R  E  B  M  U  L  P  C  A  U
E  E  R  N  A  M  L  I  A  M  Z  H  L
R  R  E  D  L  E  W  N  A  M  O  E  Y
```

RIVETER

SINGER

TEACHER

UROLOGIST

VETERINARIAN

WELDER

X-RAY (technician)

YEOMAN

ZOOLOGIST

Answers on page 182.

Eleven Coins

Among 11 coins of the same denomination, 1 is known to be counterfeit. Using a simple 2-pan balance, determine in 2 weighings if the fake is heavier or lighter than a true coin.

Star Power

LOGIC   COMPUTATION   ATTENTION

Fill in each of the empty squares in the grid so that each star is surrounded by the numbers 1 through 8 with no repeats.

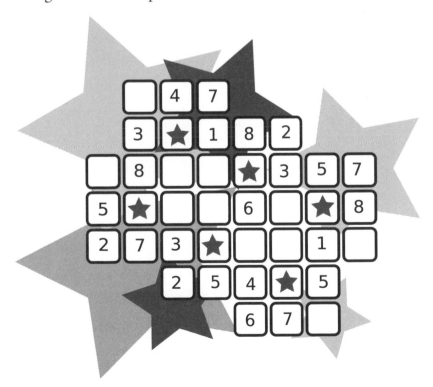

Answers on page 183.

Famous Fare

ACROSS

1. Tortoiselike
5. Word with wrench or dream
9. Medieval weapons
14. Ice shape
15. Yemeni port
16. Actress Verdugo
17. Top draft status
18. Furnish temporarily
19. Wise legislator
20. Loved dairy product?
23. Hosp. areas
24. Voice man Blanc
25. Pianist Dame Myra
26. Lush surroundings?
27. Nairobi Trio players
29. Howard Hughes's airline
32. Frequently
35. Spread unit
36. Famous twins' birthplace
37. Comedic pastry?
40. Summer coolers
41. Attention-getter
42. Argument flaws
43. Kind of party
44. Tucked in for the night
45. Director's cry
46. The Police was one
48. Norm's bartender
49. Convened
52. Soul food dessert?

57. Pertaining to surface extent
58. Ajar, e.g.
59. Hennery
60. Recipe instruction
61. One side of a 1973 ruling
62. Whet
63. Roman social sites
64. Luge, e.g.
65. Lyric poems

DOWN

1. Twenty
2. Type of month
3. Heeds
4. Don
5. Four-time Masters champ
6. Perfect example
7. Historic Quaker
8. Prefix meaning "inside"
9. Interlocks
10. Fleshy medicinal plants
11. Heavenly
12. Cain's nephew
13. Rational
21. Certain sultanate citizen
22. Root in the stands
26. They must be covered to be real
27. Hurt plenty
28. Spring event
30. Aftermath
31. "My Cup Runneth Over" singer Ed

32. Leave out
33. Confront
34. Doctor's specialty
35. Former Davis Cup captain
36. Glaswegian, e.g.
38. Big shot
39. Tack type
44. Ushers' milieus
45. Sacked
47. Extend

48. Nobel, e.g.
49. Rose
50. Offer reparation
51. Genres
52. Entrance part
53. Diva's piece
54. Spats
55. Fall birthstone
56. Reverberate

Answers on page 183.

Granola Logic

Grunela loved granola but hated all the unnatural ingredients and artificial preservatives the big cereal companies put in their commercial granolas, so she decided to buy wholesome all-natural ingredients and make her own. Grunela went to the health food store and saw that oats cost 36 cents per ounce, raisins cost 43 cents per ounce, and almonds cost 45 cents per ounce. She bought enough of each to make a pound (16 ounces) of homemade granola. She noticed when she checked out that the total price of the ingredients meant her homemade granola would cost a reasonable 39 cents an ounce. How many ounces each of oats, raisins, and almonds did Grunela buy?

Logidoku

Use deductive logic to complete the grid so that each row, column, diagonal, irregular shape, and 3×3 box contains the numbers 1 through 9 in some order. The solution is unique.

Answers on page 183.

Holiday Anagram

Find an anagram for each of the words below, which will answer the clues. Write the correct anagram on the line by each clue. When completed correctly, the first letter of the anagrams will spell the name of a U.S. holiday.

ARGENT CRANE DANGER OKAYED TINSEL SEDAN
HAYDN DEARTH ANNIE CANTER MISLED LOVELY

CLUES

1. Used in sewing
2. Useful
3. South American mountains
4. Mother-of-pearl
5. Knocked out
6. Made a happy face
7. Plant
8. Small bays
9. _____ ball
10. Senseless
11. Drink for the gods
12. Precious stone

ANSWERS

_____

_____

_____

_____

_____

_____

_____

_____

_____

_____

_____

_____

U.S. holiday:_____

Answers on page 183.

Big Screen Letter Box

The letters in Marx can be found in boxes 1, 2, 11, and 20, but not necessarily in that order. The same is true for the other actors' names indicated. Insert all the letters of the alphabet into the boxes. If you do this correctly, the shaded cells will reveal 2 more film stars.

1	2	3	4	5	6	7	8	9	10	11	12	13

14	15	16	17	18	19	20	21	22	23	24	25	26

BULLOCK: 6, 7, 15, 19, 21, 26

CLIFT: 7, 8, 13, 16, 19

DE NIRO: 3, 6, 8, 9, 20, 24

GIBSON: 3, 4, 6, 8, 15, 18

JACKSON: 3, 4, 5, 6, 11, 19, 26

KIDMAN: 1, 3, 8, 11, 24, 26

MARX: 1, 2, 11, 20

McQUEEN: 1, 3, 9, 19, 21, 25

PACINO: 3, 6, 8, 11, 17, 19

SCHWARZENEGGER: 3, 4, 9, 11, 12, 18, 19, 20, 22, 23

SMITH: 1, 4, 8, 16, 23

VALENTINO: 3, 6, 7, 8, 9, 10, 11, 16

WAYNE: 3, 9, 11, 12, 14

Answers on page 183.

Magic Square

Place the numbers 1 through 25 in the
empty squares so that all the rows, columns,
and diagonals add up to the same sum.
Each number is used only once.

17		1	8	
23				16
	6			22
	12	19	21	
11		25		9

Crypto-Quote

Cryptograms are messages in substitution code. Break the code to read the message.
For example, THE SMART CAT might become FVO QWGDF JGF if **F** is
substituted for **T, V** for **H, O** for **E,** and so on.

"ALTCT BCT ADK ALEFSJ ALBA BCT IKCT

GEMMENOPA ALBF IBREFS BF BMATC—GEFFTC

JUTTNL: NPEIWEFS B DBPP DLENL EJ PTBFEFS

AKDBCG VKO BFG REJJEFS B SECP DLK EJ

PTBFEFS BDBV MCKI VKO."

—DEFJAKF NLOCNLEPP

Answers on page 183.

123

Word Columns

Find the hidden phrase by using the letters directly below each of the blank squares. Each letter is used only once.

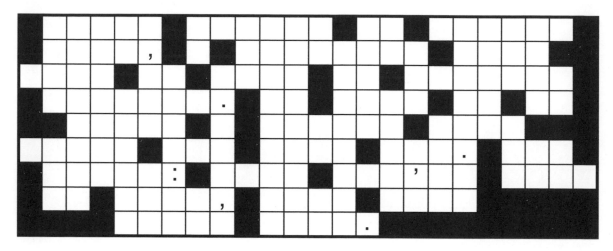

```
                        k  h
      f     m           o  n     t
   o  u  t  b  o        s  d     p     y        r
   e  o  n  t  u  u  t  h     e  n  u  y  o  u     u  e     f  r
   A  l  n  e  i  l  l  W  i  u  e  t  e  n  o  e  a  m  e  u  e
   r  o  l  g  r  l  g  a  h  h  e  n  t  e  h  t  m  i  t  o  e  p
   l  o  r  a  s  n  n  d  m  H  u  g  t  a  p  i  c  l  i  T  n  d
f  b  u  t  r  l  o  a  g  o  o  e  o  k  a  i  s  t  a  t  i  h  e
a  m  f  a  l  i  a  e  a  t  s  h  n  h  e  r  n  r  n  r  t  u  l  l
```

Answers on page 183.

Letter Quilt

Each row and column contains the letters **A, B, C, D,** and 2 empty squares. Each letter and number indicator refers to the first or second of the 4 letters encountered when reading inward. Can you complete the grid?

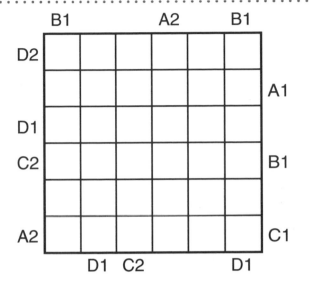

Word Ladders

Change just 1 letter on each line to go from the top word to the bottom word. Do not change the order of the letters. You must have a common English word at each step.

1. RIVET

_____

_____ a classic dog's name

_____

_____ a structure used to support growing plants

_____

TOWEL

2. BADGER

_____

_____ Macbeth thought he saw one

_____

_____ where baby Jesus slept

_____

BANNER

Answers on page 184.

Mirror, Mirror

Find the 22 things that are different between the first picture and its upside-down companion. No fair turning the picture right-side up!

Answers on page 184.

Acrostic Anagram

Unscramble the words below, then transfer the corresponding letters to the grid. When you're finished, you'll be rewarded with a quote from Sir John Vanbrugh.

1 D	2 I	3 D	4 A	5 D	6 E	■	7 G	8 C	■	9 G	10 A	11 I	■	12 E	13 H	14 F	■	15 I	16 A
17 H	18 E	19 I	20 B	■	21 G	22 E	23 B	24 E	25 B	26 D	■	27 A	■	28 A	29 H	30 E	31 A	32 F	33 C
34 B	35 C	■	36 B	37 C	■	38 E	39 I	40 A	41 G	42 F	■	43 G	44 I	45 H	46 A	■	47 G	48 F	49 H
50 A	51 B	■	52 C	53 C	54 C	55 E	56 F	57 A	58 F	59 C	60 A	61 G	62 H	63 I	■	64 B	65 A	66 D	67 C
■	68 A	69 I	70 B	71 D	72 C	73 F													

A. 40 60 57 27 28 31 50 68 10 65 4 16 46

— — — — — — — — — — — — —

P A N I I A T D E C A T C

B. 64 25 34 36 70 51 23 20

— — — — — — — —

I E S P R H E D

C. 53 52 35 54 33 72 37 59 8 67

— — — — — — — — — —

S U E N S E S L F U

D. 26 5 3 1 71 66

— — — — — —

R U E V S Y

E. 55 12 24 30 22 6 18 38

— — — — — — — —

D E O A R H F E

F. 73 56 32 48 58 14 42

— — — — — — —

I G S I N F H

G. 47 7 21 61 9 41 43

— — — — — — —

I N I T W T G

H. 17 49 29 62 45 13

— — — — — —

I W L W L O

I. 11 44 19 39 15 2 69 63

— — — — — — — —

T R I S Y O R O

Answers on page 184.

ABCD

Every cell in the 6×6 grid contains 1 of 4 letters: A, B, C, or D. No letter can be horizontally or vertically adjacent to itself. The tables above and to the left of the grid indicate how many times each letter appears in that column or row.

Can you complete the grid?

	A	2	2	1	1	1	2
	B	2	0	2	3	1	1
	C	1	1	2	0	3	2
A B C D	D	1	3	1	2	1	1
2 0 1 3							
1 1 3 1							
1 3 1 1							
3 1 1 1							
1 2 1 2							
1 2 2 1							

Wacky Wordies

Can you "read" the phrases below?

1. SUNT

2. ↓
33
33
33
↑

Answers on page 184.

Flower Garden Word Search

Every word listed is contained within the group of letters to the right. The words can be found in a straight line horizontally, vertically, or diagonally. The words can be read backward or forward. When you have found all the words, read the uncircled letters, from left to right, to reveal a gardening message.

```
S I S P O E R O C O N E F L O W E R
N S K O U N S H H B E E B A L M O I
A E C N M E W S R H A T E V R S G A
P V O C O S I O Y D A S M E E O I E
D O H A L R O A S C S P A N S Y B G
R L Y I L C C A R T E L D R F E N
A G L I E I Y R N O E O L E U X G A
G X L L N D P T T C R N O R P O O R
O O O T T O P E H U I Y W L S L N D
N F H I Z F O L E S L E S R K H I Y
A N N R E F P O M D A I V I R P A H
E R G E R A N I U M Y S P H A A R P
A T S O H D H V M A R I G O L D O E
```

A gardener needs _ _ _ _ _ _ _ _ _ _, _ _ _ _ _ _,
_ _ _ _ _ _ _ _ _, _ _ _ _ _ _ _ _ _ _ _,
_ _ _ _ _ _ _ _ _ _ _ _ _ _ _ _ _ _ _!

ASTER
BEE BALM
BEGONIA
CHRYSANTHEMUM
CONEFLOWER
COREOPSIS
COSMOS
CROCUS
DAFFODIL
DAISY
FERN

FOXGLOVE
GERANIUM
HOLLYHOCK
HOSTA
HYACINTH
HYDRANGEA
IRIS
LARKSPUR
LAVENDER
LILAC
MALLOW

MARIGOLD
PANSY
PEONY
PHLOX
POPPY
ROSE
SNAPDRAGON
TULIP
VIOLET

Answers on page 184.

Letter Quilt

Each row and column contains the letters **A, B, C, D,** and 2 empty squares. Each letter and number indicator refers to the first or second of the 4 letters encountered when reading inward. Can you complete the grid?

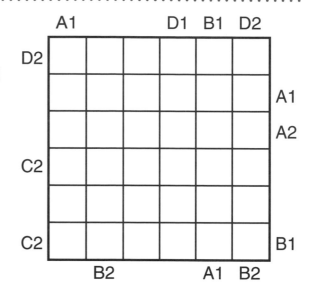

Star Power

Fill in each of the empty squares in the grid so that each star is surrounded by the numbers 1 through 8 with no repeats.

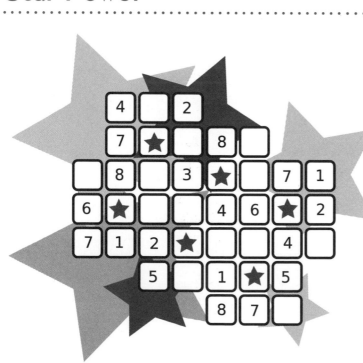

Answers on pages 184–185.

TV Documentaries

At the annual TV documentary awards, the judges have mixed up the titles of the documentaries and their directors. Although each item is in the correct column, only one item in each column is correctly positioned.

	First word	Second word	Director
1	Making	Money	Torrentino
2	Stealing	Newspapers	Spoolbag
3	Cutting	Cloth	Rodrigo
4	Eating	Bread	Alhen
5	Painting	Pizza	Capri
6	Ripping	Wallpaper	Jockson

1. Cloth is 2 places below Alhen but only 1 below Painting.
2. Ripping is 2 places below Newspapers, which is 1 place above Torrentino.
3. Capri is somewhere below Bread, which is somewhere below Stealing.
4. Making is somewhere below Cloth, which is somewhere above Jockson.
5. Rodrigo is 2 places above Wallpaper but only 1 below Cutting.

Can you find the correct first word and second word of the documentary title together with the director for each award position?

Answers on page 185.

Not in the Dairy Case

ACROSS

1. Testing site
4. Absorb, as gravy
9. Cadge
12. ___ Miss
13. Command to a lifter
14. Seek office
15. Variety of squash
17. "This American Life" host Glass
18. Net receipts?
19. Major shipbuilding city
21. "The Happy ___" (Harry Connick, Jr., holiday song)
23. It may be blonde
24. Cable TV network
27. "…and seven years ___…"
29. Emblem on Canada's flag
33. Candy bar ingredient
37. Bridge
39. "The lowest form of humour": Samuel Johnson
40. Color in Canada's flag
41. Tree used for chair seats
44. Women's article of clothing
46. Temporary window replacement, sometimes
50. Off the cuff
54. Kia subcompact
55. Fountain offering
57. Bollix
58. Take control of
59. AC/DC lead singer ___ Scott
60. Run off at the mouth
61. Classic battle participants
62. Long in the tooth

DOWN

1. Brain region
2. Reunion attendee, briefly
3. Kind of software release
4. Natural plastic
5. Done, to Donne
6. Hunger pain
7. Tongue neighbor
8. Colorful part of a plant
9. Guardhouse
10. Currency adopted by Slovenia in 2007
11. Chew like a beaver
16. Cause of sudden death?
20. Put on the market
22. E-tail?
24. Lecture no-nos
25. Thimbleful
26. Newbery Medal org.
28. Alley ending?
30. Listening device
31. Had some food
32. Gave some food to
34. Felt sure about
35. Baby lion

36. Freeway access points
42. Center of power
43. "Hack" star David
45. Promotions
46. Michael Crichton novel
47. Former currency of Turkey

48. Prince Andrew's dukedom
49. Caen couple
51. University of New Mexico athlete
52. Graven image
53. Rubber or brass follower
56. "Two heads ___ better than one"

Answers on page 185.

Euphemism Anagram

Below are 11 jumbled phrases. Each is an anagram (rearrangement) of a word or phrase that fits the story. Can you decipher all 11?

"Welcome and greetings, class!" said Professor Doublespeak. "We are gathered to discuss my favorite topic, namely those watered-down, lily-livered tergiversations known as euphemisms. Also known as weasel words, hedges, waffles, and equivocations. A euphemism is the substitution of milder, gentler, 'kinder' word or phrase for a blunter, more candid one.

"We no longer speak plainly," the professor went on. "Example one: Did any of you grow up in a trailer? Perhaps. But do you call it a trailer now? Of course not—it's an **OHIO EMBLEM**.

"Example the second: Do any of your parents have false teeth? Or do they have **RED TUNES**?

"Another instance, and then it's your turn. Does anyone here drive a used car? Or is it a **PROVIDENCE WHEEL**? And who else can offer a euphemistic phrase?"

A girl in the front row raised her hand. "How about when you buy undies?" she giggled. "Now they're 'lingerie,' or **BLUE MINNESOTAN**!"

Another student piped up. "What about when you take your trash to the garbage dump?" he said. "Now they call it **ALL TIN FAIRYLANDS**."

"Does anyone go to prison anymore?" asked another. "No, he's sent to a **FICTIONAL CAROLOER CITY**!"

"How about a kid who's too lazy to do his homework?" a student offered. "He's not lazy, he's a **VIDEO MUTANT**!"

Everyone was getting into the act. "If you go to the gym, do you work up a good sweat?" asked one. "No, you work up a lot of **OPEN AIRSTRIP**!"

"Is there such a thing as an old person anymore? No, he's a **TIN CORN SEIZER**!"

"We ran out of toilet paper at our house last week," said the girl in the front row. "But nobody says 'toilet paper' anymore. It's **BOISTEROUS MATH**!"

Professor Doublespeak was delighted with the fine response from his class. "Well done, my friends!" he said. "You've done so well that I'm going to cut the class short. And, to tell you the truth, I have to go to the **LOBOTOMY LISTER**."

Answers on page 185.

Math Grid

Fill each square in the grid with a digit from 1 through 9. When the numbers in each row are multiplied, you should arrive at the total in the right-hand column. When the numbers in each column are multiplied, you should arrive at the total on the bottom line. The numbers in each diagonal must multiply to the totals in the upper and lower right corners.

						16
5	1		3	4		480
3		5		1	4	480
4	4		1	2	2	192
	3	4	2		1	288
1		4	5	3		360
	5	3		1	4	120
120	240	2880	240	144	192	720

Word Ladders

Change just 1 letter on each line to go from the top word to the bottom word. Do not change the order of the letters. You must have a common English word at each step.

1. CLUSTER

_____

_____ a workman employed to use explosives

_____

_____ serving dish

PLANTER

2. GREAT

_____ snack

_____

_____

_____ a domesticated subspecies

_____

GREET

Answers on page 185.

Anagram Place

Find an anagram for each of the words below, which will answer the clues. Write the correct anagram on the line by each clue. When completed correctly, the first letter of the anagrams will spell the name of a U.S. location.

APPEND AUSTEN CRIES DOYLE PEACH
RIATA ROMAN SLINK SNEAK STONE
TACIT TENOR TORTE UNWARY

CLUES

ANSWERS

1. Airport path _____

2. Aquatic mammal _____

3. Inexpensive _____

4. Pottery ovens _____

5. Swiss call _____

6. Large country house _____

7. Start _____

8. Dethrone _____

9. _____ Dame _____

10. Small crown _____

11. Top floor of a house _____

12. Cake decorators _____

13. Slept _____

14. Rattle _____ _____

U.S. location:_____

Answers on page 185.

Good-Looking Logic

Five good-looking guys went shopping at the Gadgets for Good-Looking Guys electronics store. Each good-looking guy walked out of Gadgets for Good-Looking Guys with a different electronic gadget for his good-looking home. Each good-looking guy went to his good-looking home and installed his electronic gadget in a different room of the house than the other good-looking guys did. Here's some of the things the good-looking guys did:

Mr. Clooney did not install his gadget in his bedroom.

Mr. Depp bought a PC.

Tom installed his gadget in his bathroom.

Mr. Cruise bought a robot vacuum.

Johnny bought a global positioning system.

Tom did not install his gadget in his bedroom.

George did not buy a DVD player.

Matt installed his gadget in his kitchen.

Johnny did not install his gadget in his living room.

Mr. Pitt installed his gadget in his attic.

Mr. Damon did not install his gadget in his kitchen.

Brad bought a wide-screen TV.

What was each good-looking guy's first and last name, what electronic gadget did each buy, and in what room of their good-looking house did each install his gadget?

Answers on page 185.

Acrostic Anagram

Unscramble the words below, then transfer the corresponding letters to the grid. When you're finished, you'll be rewarded with a quote from Simone Weil.

1 E		2 D	3 A	4 D	5 F	6 F	7 H	8 C		9 A	10 E	11 F		12 B	13 C		14 A	15 I	16 H
	17 E	18 F	19 A	20 D	21 G	22 G	23 E	24 D	25 E	26 A	27 A	28 D		29 G	30 B		31 I	32 D	33 F
34 B	35 A	36 E		37 D	38 C		39 I	40 E	41 A		42 C	43 H	44 C	45 E	46 G	47 B	48 E	49 I	50 I
51 C	52 A		53 I	54 E	55 C	56 A	57 C		58 G	59 A		60 A	61 F	62 F	63 F		64 D	65 H	
66 A	67 I	68 B	69 B	70 F	71 A	72 H	73 F	74 B											

A. 56 66 3 52 14 59 35 60 19 71 9 26 27 41

___ ___ ___ ___ ___ ___ ___ ___ ___ ___ ___ ___ ___ ___

R E E O U C B N N C L T A A

B. 47 30 74 69 12 34 68

___ ___ ___ ___ ___ ___ ___

R O E D S I S

C. 44 51 8 42 38 55 13 57

___ ___ ___ ___ ___ ___ ___ ___

D I H F G O L S

D. 32 2 37 4 20 64 28 24

___ ___ ___ ___ ___ ___ ___ ___

R E R O N T H I

E. 54 23 48 45 17 1 10 40 25 36

___ ___ ___ ___ ___ ___ ___ ___ ___ ___

A R C A E H S E H T

F. 5 33 73 18 61 62 6 11 70 63

___ ___ ___ ___ ___ ___ ___ ___ ___ ___

A E E H F R R E T T

G. 58 46 22 29 21

___ ___ ___ ___ ___

F A T W S

H. 72 16 65 7 43

___ ___ ___ ___ ___

U E N E V

I. 53 50 39 15 31 67 49

___ ___ ___ ___ ___ ___ ___

T I T H W O U

Answers on page 185.

Red, White, and Blue

Each row, column, and long diagonal contains 2 reds, 2 whites, and 2 blues. From the clues given, can you complete the grid?

Hint: Write the possibilities in small letters until a picture emerges. For example: "The blues are between the whites" means that the 2 outside squares can be only red or white. Don't forget that the 2 long diagonals contain only 2 cells of each color.

```
   A B C D E F
1
2
3
4
5
6
```

1. The blues are adjacent.
2. Each white is immediately to the left of each red.
3. Both the whites are somewhere between both the reds.
4. No clue needed.
5. Both the reds are somewhere between both the whites
6. Both the whites are somewhere between both the blues.

A. The whites are adjacent.
B. No clue needed.
C. Both the whites are somewhere between both the blues.
D. No clue needed.
E. One white is bounded by 2 reds, the other by 2 blues.
F. No clue needed.

Answers on page 186.

Big Top Code-doku

Solve this puzzle just as you do a sudoku. Use deductive logic to complete the grid so that each row, each column, and each 3×3 box contains 1 of the letters of the anagram IT'S NO MEAL. The solution is unique. When you have completed the puzzle, the shaded squares can be read top to bottom, from left to right, to form a phrase describing something you might see at the circus.

			O	I				
			S	M				
	L	T						
				T		O		I
S						E		
		A		I				
	O	L						
		S		E	M		A	
A	T				L			

Hidden message:_____

Puzzling Series

Can you complete this series?

SEPTFS

Answers on page 186.

Living Large Anagram

Below are 10 jumbled phrases. Each is an anagram (rearrangement) of a word or phrase that fits the story. Can you decipher all 10?

At the Museum of UnamBIGuously Large Things, a seven-foot docent addressed the group of tourists.

"We like to think big," he said. "Our favorite biblical person is **HOT GAIL**. Our favorite animal is **THE PLANE**. Our favorite geographical unit is **CNN TONITE**."

"What's your favorite vehicle?" a tourist asked.

"The **OSTRICH MELT**, of course," the docent grinned.

"How about your favorite tourist attraction?" ventured another sightseer.

"The **LEO MUSIC**, naturally! Now please follow me as I point out some other big things. Here, for instance, is a model of our favorite ocean-going vessel, the **SUSIE CHIRP**. And in this display you see our most revered athletes, **NO EMOLLIENT FLAB**. Although we surely give props to the **MEOW RUSTLERS** as well! Over here you can see a satellite view of that glorious hole in the ground, the **NANCY DRAGON**. And finally," he said, concluding the tour, "on that wall you see the **END BATTALION**, a large number that gets larger every second. I must admit that it is not one of our favorite things... but it is, as they say, totally ginormous!"

Trivia on the Brain
The brain continues to produce neurons throughout almost its entire life— even into the seventies!

Answers on page 186.

U.S. Presidents Letter Box

The letters in POLK can be found in boxes 7, 8, 13, and 23, but not necessarily in that order. Similarly, the letters in all the other names can be found in the boxes indicated. Your task is to insert all the letters of the alphabet into the boxes. If you do this correctly, the shaded cells will reveal 2 more U.S. presidents.

1	2	3	4	5	6	7	8	9	10	11	12	13

14	15	16	17	18	19	20	21	22	23	24	25	26
												Z

BUCHANAN: 2, 5, 10, 19, 20, 22

CARTER: 4, 5, 9, 10, 25

CLEVELAND: 1, 2, 5, 7, 10, 18, 25

FILLMORE: 7, 8, 9, 11, 12, 14, 25

JEFFERSON: 2, 3, 8, 9, 11, 21, 25

McKINLEY: 2, 6, 7, 10, 12, 14, 23, 25

NIXON: 2, 8, 12, 24

POLK: 7, 8, 13, 23

QUINCY ADAMS: 2, 5, 6, 10, 12, 14, 16, 18, 20, 21

REAGAN: 2, 5, 9, 17, 25

WASHINGTON: 2, 4, 5, 8, 12, 15, 17, 21, 22

Answers on page 186.

Nice Pets

In the Best Behaved Pet competition, the prize winners were about to be announced. Unfortunately, the judges have all their results wrongly recorded. Although each item is in the correct column, only 1 item in each column is correctly positioned.

	Owner	Pet	Name
1	Arthur	cat	Keith
2	Bob	rhino	Len
3	Cathy	pig	Molly
4	Dennis	crocodile	Norma
5	Evelyn	leopard	Olive

1. The leopard is 2 places below Keith.
2. Arthur is 2 places above the crocodile.
3. Norma is 2 places above Evelyn.
4. Dennis is 3 places below Len.
5. The rhino is not in first place.

Can you find the owner, pet, and pet name for each?

Answers on page 186.

Math Grid

Fill each square in the grid with a digit from 1 through 9. When the numbers in each row are added, you should arrive at the total in the right-hand column. When the numbers in each column are added, you should arrive at the total on the bottom line. The numbers in each diagonal must add up to the totals in the upper and lower right corners.

									48
1	5	3	6	7	4	9		8	50
4			4	3	5		6	9	46
9	8	3		1	5	4		7	46
	3	4	4		3	5	5	9	43
1	9	3		7		6	7		45
8	2		4	3	9		4	5	49
7		3		3	7	8		4	48
2	4		8	2		3	2		40
	8	3	7		6	8	5		53
49	47	40	51	32	42	58	39	62	39

Wacky Wordy

Can you "read" the phrase below?

M+UP

Answers on page 186.

Painterly Logic

Painter Pat has been hired to paint the walls, doors, and roofs (yes, roofs!) of the brand new trailers in Prefabulous, the world's tackiest trailer park, where it seems that each owner wants their walls, doors, and roofs to be painted with 3 different colors from the colors of the rainbow. Being individualists, the owners also want their doors, walls, and roofs to be painted different color combinations from their neighbors, with every trailer using 3 colors. Painter Pat arrived at the park and saw that the trailers are addressed 101 through 105 as they line up consecutively on Paisley Way. The colors the owners asked him to use to paint the walls, doors, and roofs of their trailers are red, orange, yellow, green, blue, indigo, and violet. None of the owners were home, but they left the following instructions for Pat.

The owner who wants orange doors and indigo walls does not live in Trailer Number 103.

The owner of Trailer 103 wants a green roof.

The owner of Trailer 102 wants yellow walls and a red roof.

The owner of Trailer 105 wants red doors.

The owner who wants the walls of his trailer painted orange and the roof blue lives directly next door to the owner who wants his trailer painted with green doors and violet walls.

What colors did Painter Pat paint the walls, doors, and roofs of each trailer?

Trivia on the Brain

Only 4 weeks after conception, a human embryo's brain is developing at an astonishing rate. At this stage the first brain cells in the body, neurons, are forming at a rate of 250,000 every minute!

Answers on page 186.

Herbs and Spices

LANGUAGE

This story is a mixed-up foray into plants that are tasty or medicinal or both. There are 9 jumbled phrases. Each is an anagram (rearragement) of a word or phrase that fits the story. Can you decipher all 9?

Guiding a group of young herbalists-in-training through the Herb Museum, the veteran botanist stopped at a display of plants that looked like angry hedgehogs. "Here we have **AACHEN ICE**, which is not really ice from Aachen. It's a group of spiny-looking plants called Purple Coneflowers.

"Be careful not to confuse it with this other herb, **HARD PEE**, with which it shares four letters," he said, pointing to a plant also known as *ma huang* or Mormon Tea.

"And over here we have **EGGS INN**, a controversial herb often found in energy drinks and believed by many to have aphrodisiac powers. Right next to it, this herb that somewhat resembles a fern, is **RAN ALIVE**, sometimes called all-heal. It's used for sedation and antianxiety effects.

"Over here," he went on, "is **MY FORCE**, a fast-growing perennial that had a wealth of medicinal uses in earlier days. Today, organic farmers use it as a fertilizer.

"And in this case is **MAD KAREN**, a member of the nightshade family, long used in magic rituals because its roots are thought to resemble the human figure, both male and female.

"Here," he said, pointing to plants on a table, "is **NEHRU HOOD**, a hardy, bushy plant used as an expectorant and tonic.

"Finally, on the next table, is **CLAIM HOME**, an annual plant of the sunflower family, which can be used as an herbal tea or a gentle sleep aid.

"That concludes our tour," the botanist said, leading the students to a picnic table. "Please help yourselves to some cookies and **NATIONAL DEED**!"

Answers on page 186.

Logidoku

Use deductive logic to complete the grid so that each row, column, diagonal, irregular shape, and 3×3 box contains the numbers 1 through 9 in some order. The solution is unique.

Genius Logic

Al Gibra wants to attend a meeting of the super-exclusive Mathematical Geniuses Club, but he doesn't know the secret password that would get him past the bouncer, who looks like a really buff Albert Einstein. Al decided to hide behind some bushes and see if he could figure out the secret admission code. A wild-haired man approached the door. The doorman said, "What is the square root of sixteen?" "Seven," replied the man, and the bouncer let him in. Al was confused. How could a genius give the wrong answer and still get in? A man in a white lab coat was next. The doorman asked him, "Seven goes into seven hundred how many times?" "Eight," replied the man, and the doorman let him in. Al was shocked. A woman carrying a tiny computer walked up. The doorman said, "Two plus two." "Three," replied the woman, and the doorman let her in. The meeting was about to start, and Al still didn't know the code. He decided to take a chance and walked up to the door. The doorman said, "Five squared." Al replied, "Twenty-five." "Wrong!" yelled the doorman and shooed Al away. What answer should Al have given that would have allowed him admittance into the Mathematical Geniuses Club?

Answers on page 187.

147

Math Grid

Fill each square in the grid with a digit from 1 through 9. When the numbers in each row are added, you should arrive at the total in the right-hand column. When the numbers in each column are added, you should arrive at the total on the bottom line. The numbers in each diagonal must add up to the totals in the upper and lower right corners.

										72
3		7	7	5	6	8	1	9		57
3	6		5	6	9		9		6	64
4	5			9	8	5	7		2	61
6		4	6		7	9	9		5	64
9		6		7		2	8	4	9	64
	7	8	3		5		9	7		58
6	5	8		3	4	7		9	4	57
	5		6	8	3		9		1	55
8	7	5		6	2	5		8		62
3		7	5		1	6	5	4		49
48	61	67	65	63	51	55	62	68	51	62

Crypto-Quote

Cryptograms are messages in substitution code. Break the code to read the message. For example, THE SMART CAT might become FVO QWGDF JGF if **F** is substituted for **T**, **V** for **H**, **O** for **E**, and so on.

"ACO RBHDA ILP JEDA BJFEHAILA ACBLK ER INN,

IA NOIDA REH GHBAOHD AEPIM, BD AE DAHBF

NILKVIKO SNOIL, AE NIM BA TIHO PEGL AE ACO

TELO."   —OHLODA COJBLKGIM

Answers on page 187.

Oh, Waiter!

There's a fly in his soup! Go pick up the soup, take it back to the chef, pick up the new bowl, and get back to the hungry patron while the soup is still hot.

START ▶

FINISH ▼

Answer on page 187.

Tree Tops

LANGUAGE GENERAL KNOWLEDGE

ACROSS

1. Gossip
4. Self-righteous person
8. ___ jure (by the law itself)
12. Hurry-scurry
13. Heckelphone cousin
14. Housekeeper
15. Body of lawyers
16. Colonial pattern of hospitality
18. Flightless bird
20. Certain bead makeup
21. Leader with no responsibilities
25. Resistance to change
26. Safecrackers
30. Uplifting attire
31. Shoot down
33. Sénat vote?
34. Montenegro dwellers
37. Frog variety
40. Popular name for a home-repair product
42. Sudden attack
44. Drivel
45. Rubbery candy
48. Maryland's state tree
51. "My Girl" star Chlumsky
52. It may be a penny
53. Yonder yacht
54. Peel off
55. June 6, 1944
56. Graffiti signature

DOWN

1. Quick punch
2. Oklahoma headquarters of the Chickasaw Nation
3. Drive in the form of a screw
4. Roy Lichtenstein's genre
5. What you get for driving someone home (abbr.)
6. Former Romanian president Iliescu
7. Amelia and Abigail Gabble in "The Aristocats"
8. Prevent
9. He got a brand new bag, in song
10. Reservoir deposit
11. Poetric tribute
17. Not toward
19. Dickens's "___ Mutual Friend"
21. Misinformation pieces
22. Concerning
23. Teutonic article
24. First name in Rastafari movement
27. One of 4 on a football field
28. Mentor
29. Competing team
32. Gen ___
35. Nickname giver on ESPN
36. Dispatch
38. Large bird of prey
39. European Tour grp.
41. Substitute for "mea culpa"
42. Grand ___ Railroad

43. Dodge car

45. Subject of Boyle's law

46. Stop running

47. "One Day ___ Time" (TV series)

49. Epiphany exclamation

50. Beer container

Answers on page 187.

Acrostic Anagram

Unscramble the words below, then transfer the corresponding letters to the grid. When you're finished, you'll be rewarded with a quote from Virginia Woolf.

1 D	2 G		3 E	4 H	5 B	6 B	7 D	8 H		9 B	10 A	11 D	12 A		13 G		14 A	15 A	16 D
17 B	18 A	19 C	20 G	21 H	22 F	23 G		24 C	25 A		26 E		27 B	28 F	29 H	30 A		31 C	32 A
33 E	34 E	35 G	36 B		37 H	38 B	39 F	40 C		41 C	42 H		43 B	44 G	45 E	46 G	47 G	48 G	49 G
	50 C	51 F	52 A	53 E		54 E	55 B		56 F	57 A	58 E	59 F	60 C	61 H		62 H	63 D	64 D	65 D
	66 E		67 F	68 F	69 E	70 B	71 A	72 A											

A. 14 15 18 10 52 72 57 32 12 71 25 30

__ __ __ __ __ __ __ __ __ __ __ __

E P E E D A R R P S S N

B. 17 27 38 5 70 55 9 36 6 43

__ __ __ __ __ __ __ __ __ __

S U F O L O H S P E

C. 40 31 50 24 41 60 19

__ __ __ __ __ __ __

N I O S M O T

D. 63 16 7 1 64 11 65

__ __ __ __ __ __ __

O O O N N T P

E. 66 3 26 58 69 45 54 33 34 53

__ __ __ __ __ __ __ __ __ __

A A N A P T O I T D

F. 67 22 39 28 51 59 68 56

__ __ __ __ __ __ __ __

R E D H A F E O

G. 48 13 46 47 23 2 35 20 44 49

__ __ __ __ __ __ __ __ __ __

R U N O L A Y E V S

H. 8 21 37 42 62 29 4 61

__ __ __ __ __ __ __ __

S F D I U D F E

Answers on page 187.

Star Power

Fill in each of the empty squares in the grid so that each star is surrounded by the numbers 1 through 8 with no repeats.

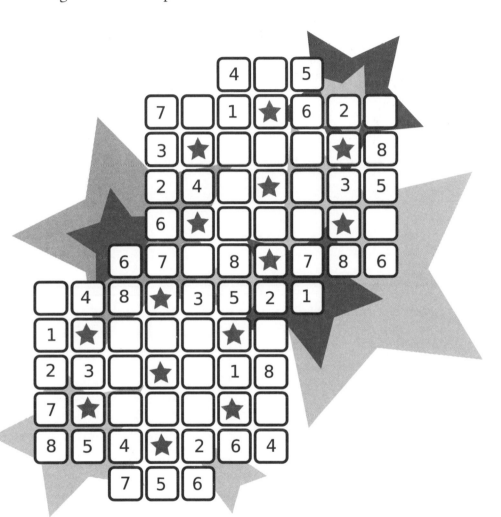

Answers on page 188.

153

Word Jigsaw

Fit the pieces into the frame to form common, uncapitalized words reading across and down crossword-style. There's no need to rotate the pieces; they'll fit as shown, with each piece used exactly once.

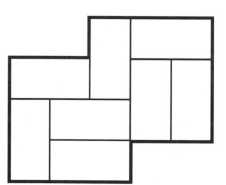

Move It!

Can you move 1 line in this sequence to create a new word?

BPAVQ

Answers on page 188.

Hashi

Each circle represents an island, with the number inside indicating the number of bridges connected to it. Draw bridges between islands using the number given, but there can be no more than 2 bridges going in the same direction and there must be a continuous path connecting all islands. Bridges can only be vertical or horizontal and may not cross islands or other bridges.

② ③   ③ ③ ③
    ② ② ①
① ②   ③   ②
       ③ ③
② ③ ④   ②
       ③   ②
  ② ③ ④   ④
⑤   ② ①
  ①   ② ④ ③

③ ② ③ ② ②
  ②   ③ ② ③

Number Crossword

Fill in this crossword with numbers instead of letters. Use the clues to determine which of the numbers 1 through 9 belongs in each square. No zeros are used.

ACROSS

  1. A multiple of 11
  3. 1-Across times (1 plus 2-Down)
  5. Its first digit is the sum of its last 3 digits
  6. A square number that ends in the same digit as 1-Across

DOWN

  1. A square number
  2. A square number
  3. Its last digit is the sum of its first 2 digits
  4. Consecutive digits, descending

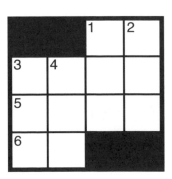

Answers on page 188.

Big Top Code-doku

Solve this puzzle just as you do a sudoku. Use deductive logic to complete the grid so that each row, each column, and each 3×3 box contains 1 of the letters of the anagram MY CPA HERD. The solution is unique. When you have completed the puzzle, the shaded squares can be read top to bottom, from left to right, to form a phrase describing something you might see at the circus.

Hidden message: _____

_____

	D		C		P	M		
					H	R		
E								
				E				A
P	H	A						
			A		M		D	
	C	Y					M	
	P			M	Y		C	
	R	H	P					

Word Ladders

Change just 1 letter on each line to go from the top word to the bottom word. Do not change the order of the letters. You must have a common English word at each step.

1. RHYME

_____

_____ add an s for a London river

_____

_____ Bond preferred it if the bartender did this to his martini

_____

_____

STALL

2. GRIME

_____

_____

_____ thick and messy liquid

_____

_____

SWIPE

Answers on page 188.

156

Wild West

The Western cattle trail was notorious for murder among the cowhands. The leader noted the deaths of the 6 hands who were shot on the journey, but on reaching his destination he found that he had mixed up the order and details of those who died. Although each item is in the correct column, only 1 entry in each column is correctly positioned.

	Name	Surname	Location	Firearm
1	Abel	Garrett	San Antonio	Schofield
2	Butch	Hitchcock	Fort Griffin	Peacemaker
3	Cat	Indiana	Dodge City	Derringer
4	Drew	James	Ogallala	Cavalry
5	Earp	Kid	Colby	Winchester
6	Fingers	Lightning	Red River	Golden Boy

1. San Antonio is 3 places above the Golden Boy.
2. Hitchcock is somewhere above Lightning and 2 places above the Derringer.
3. Earp is 2 places below Fort Griffin.
4. Kid is 1 row below both Butch and Colby.
5. Fingers is immediately below Earp but 3 places below Garrett.
6. Butch is 1 row below the Winchester and somewhere above Cat.
7. The Peacemaker is 2 rows above Dodge City.

Can you find the correct name, surname, location of the murder, and firearm used for each?

Answers on page 188.

Fitting Words

In this miniature crossword, the clues are listed randomly and are numbered for convenience only. It is up to you to figure out the placement of the 9 answers. To help you out, we've inserted 1 letter in the grid, and this is the only occurrence of that letter in the puzzle.

CLUES

1. Wide-eyed
2. Radiant
3. Fairy-tale meanies
4. Farm females
5. Two-door car
6. Easy gait
7. Dining room furniture
8. Mexican snack
9. Become hazy

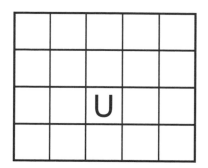

Cross Math

Fill in the grid using the numbers 1 through 9 only once.

	+		-		=	10
+		-		-		
	+		+		=	10
-		+		+		
	×		-		=	10
=		=		=		
10		11		10		

Answers on page 188.

Red, White, Blue, and Green

Each row, column, and long diagonal contains 2 reds, 2 whites, 2 blues, and 2 greens. From the clues given, can you complete the grid?

```
     A  B  C  D  E  F  G  H
  1 ┌──┬──┬──┬──┬──┬──┬──┬──┐
    │  │  │  │  │  │  │  │  │
  2 ├──┼──┼──┼──┼──┼──┼──┼──┤
    │  │  │  │  │  │  │  │  │
  3 ├──┼──┼──┼──┼──┼──┼──┼──┤
    │  │  │  │  │  │  │  │  │
  4 ├──┼──┼──┼──┼──┼──┼──┼──┤
    │  │  │  │  │  │  │  │  │
  5 ├──┼──┼──┼──┼──┼──┼──┼──┤
    │  │  │  │  │  │  │  │  │
  6 ├──┼──┼──┼──┼──┼──┼──┼──┤
    │  │  │  │  │  │  │  │  │
  7 ├──┼──┼──┼──┼──┼──┼──┼──┤
    │  │  │  │  │  │  │  │  │
  8 └──┴──┴──┴──┴──┴──┴──┴──┘
```

1. Two whites, a red, and a green are directly enclosed by both the blues.
2. Three different colors are directly enclosed by both the blues.
3. The reds are separated by 6 cells; the greens are adjacent.
4. No clue needed.
5. Two whites, a green, and a red are directly enclosed by both the blues.
6. The whites are separated by 6 cells; the greens are not adjacent.
7. The reds are not adjacent.
8. There are no blues or reds in cells A, B, C, or D.
A. Two reds, 2 whites, and a green are directly enclosed by both the blues.
B. The blues are adjacent; the whites are adjacent.
C. No clue needed.
D. No clue needed.
E. No clue needed.
F. Each blue is immediately above each red; the whites are not adjacent.
G. One green is directly enclosed by both the blues.
H. The pattern of colors takes the form abacdcdb.

Answers on page 189.

Acrostic Anagram

Unscramble the words below, then transfer the corresponding letters to the grid. When you're finished, you'll be rewarded with a quote from Voltaire.

1 F	2 I	3 E	■	4 I	5 I	6 A	7 G	8 H	■	9 H	10 G	11 A	12 F	13 G	14 D	15 G	16 I	17 F	18 D
19 G	■	20 C	21 C	■	22 F	23 B	24 I	■	25 E	■	26 A	27 F	28 E	29 E	30 I	31 E	■	32 C	33 B
34 A	35 B	36 C	■	37 H	38 H	39 C	40 B	■	41 G	42 E	43 I	44 D	■	45 C	46 B	47 D	48 F	49 H
50 D	51 B	52 G	53 D	54 E	55 E	■	56 A	57 D	58 H	■	59 C	60 G	61 G	■	62 I	63 H	■	64 D	65 H
66 F	67 F	68 B	69 A	70 A	71 I	72 H	73 F												

A. 69 70 26 56 11 6 34

_ _ _ _ _ _ _

AMBEACR

B. 46 23 40 68 33 35 51

_ _ _ _ _ _ _

NHAXTAR

C. 45 59 39 20 36 21 32

_ _ _ _ _ _ _

DHMAEMW

D. 64 50 53 47 18 14 57 44

_ _ _ _ _ _ _ _

ERSWNSET

E. 54 42 25 29 28 3 55 31

_ _ _ _ _ _ _ _

NHETNTIS

F. 67 22 66 12 73 27 48 1 17

_ _ _ _ _ _ _ _ _

ACATSTRAC

G. 60 7 15 13 10 52 19 41 61

_ _ _ _ _ _ _ _ _

SSTAIRLMA

H. 49 63 37 38 72 65 58 9 8

_ _ _ _ _ _ _ _ _

DHODAHETE

I. 2 30 5 24 4 43 62 71 16

_ _ _ _ _ _ _ _ _

DNHOWSIKO

Answers on page 189.

Word Jigsaw

Fit the pieces into the frame to form common, uncapitalized words reading across and down crossword-style. There's no need to rotate the pieces; they'll fit as shown, with each piece used exactly once.

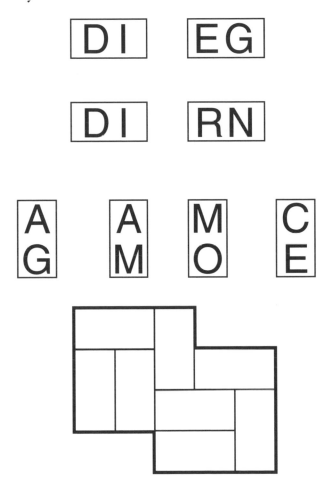

Trivia on the Brain

The Latin word for tree bark is "cortex." The cortex protects your brain just as bark protects the inside of a tree.

Answers on page 189.

Star Power

Fill in each of the empty squares in the grid so that each star is surrounded by the numbers 1 through 8 with no repeats.

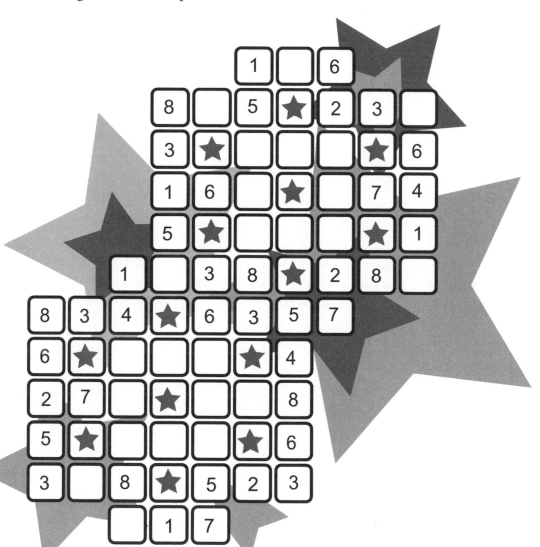

Answers on page 189.

Hashi

LOGIC SPATIAL PLANNING

Each circle represents an island, with the number inside indicating the number of bridges connected to it. Draw bridges between islands using the number given, but there can be no more than 2 bridges going in the same direction and there must be a continuous path connecting all islands. Bridges can only be vertical or horizontal and may not cross islands or other bridges.

Cross Math

LOGIC COMPUTATION

Fill in the grid using the numbers 1 through 9 only once.

	+		÷		=	2
-		-		+		
	X		X		=	24
+		-		X		
	-		+		=	4
=		=		=		
3		4		20		

Answers on page 189.

163

Word Columns

Find the hidden phrase by using the letters directly below each of the blank squares. Each letter is used only once.

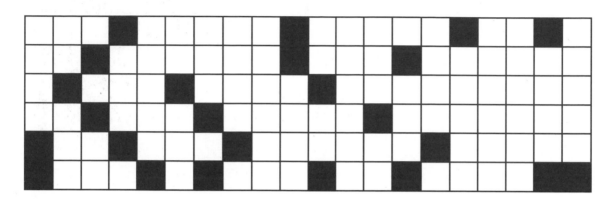

```
                    y         e              e   s
        e      e v      o r      t  r    h  h i  n   g
    g o s r t t  m c i  t o n t  h t g u i  t
    e d t a s h  e e f  t e r s  t s e h i  i   n
    N f i t n a  f a a  e s u u  s i l o w  n   e
    h i o b e d  e r w  n f n o  d i s e d  c   s
```

Wacky Wordy

Can you "read" the phrase below?

G O E S

Answers on page 189.

Logidoku

Use deductive logic to complete the grid so that each row, column, diagonal, irregular shape, and 3×3 box contains the numbers 1 through 9 in some order. The solution is unique.

Fitting Words

In this miniature crossword, the clues are listed randomly and are numbered for convenience only. It is up to you to figure out the placement of the 9 answers. To help you out, we've inserted 1 letter in the grid, and this is the only occurrence of that letter in the puzzle.

CLUES

1. Reverse
2. Foal's father
3. Loosen, as shoelaces
4. Coop group
5. Knuckleheads
6. Campus rectangle
7. On
8. Festoon
9. Suppress

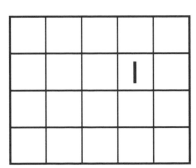

Answers on pages 189–190.

Prize Poetry

In the prize poetry competition, the judges have mixed up all their information for the prize-giving. Each item is in the correct column, but only 1 item in each column is correctly positioned.

	Name	Surname	State	Poem
1	Andrea	Grimble	Montana	Sunrise
2	Betty	Horse	Nebraska	Tolerance
3	Colin	Irvine	Ohio	Umbrella
4	Daisy	Jackson	Pennsylvania	Vanity
5	Erwin	Keats	Iowa	Waterfall
6	Francis	Lee	Colorado	Expectancy

1. Daisy is 1 place above Lee.
2. Tolerance is 1 place below Horse but 1 above Colin.
3. Pennsylvania is 2 places below Betty but 3 below Irvine.
4. Betty is not adjacent to Erwin.
5. Ohio is one place below Waterfall.
6. Erwin is 1 place above Expectancy but 2 below Montana.
7. Grimble is 1 place above Vanity but 3 above Iowa.

Can you give the candidates' correct name, surname, state of origin, and poem title for each position?

Answers on page 190.

Word Jigsaw

Fit the pieces into the frame to form common, uncapitalized words reading across and down crossword-style. There's no need to rotate the pieces; they'll fit as shown, with each piece used exactly once.

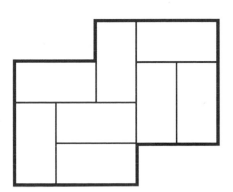

The Start of Things

Can you determine the missing letter in this progression?

I T B, G C T _ A T E

Answers on page 190.

At Peak Efficiency

Aphorism Code-doku

LOGIC **LANGUAGE**

Solve this puzzle just as you do a sudoku. Use deductive logic to complete the grid so that each row, each column, and each 3×3 box contains 1 of the letters of the anagram SUCH TANGO. The solution is unique. When you have completed the puzzle, the shaded squares will form a hidden message read top to bottom, from left to right.

Hidden message: _____

_____

			H			T		
U							A	C
		T	C		G			
T						C		A
	S	C					H	
	O						S	
				T	A			U
O						A	G	
N					O			S

Hashi

LOGIC **SPATIAL PLANNING**

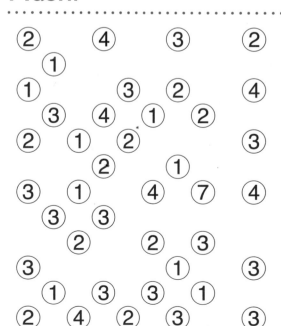

Each circle represents an island, with the number inside indicating the number of bridges connected to it. Draw bridges between islands using the number given, but there can be no more than 2 bridges going in the same direction and there must be a continuous path connecting all islands. Bridges can only be vertical or horizontal and may not cross islands or other bridges.

Answers on page 190.

168

REASSESS YOUR BRAIN

You have just completed a set of puzzles selected to challenge your various mental skills. We hope you enjoyed them. And did the mental exercise you engaged in also improve your memory, attention, problem-solving, and other important cognitive skills? In order to find out, please fill out this questionnaire. It is exactly the same as the one you filled out before you embarked on our puzzles. So now you will be in a position to compare your cognitive skills before and after you challenged them with cognitive exercise. The real question is whether solving our puzzles had a real impact on your real-life performance. We hope it did.

The questions below are designed to test your skills in the areas of memory, problem-solving, creative thinking, attention, language, and more. Please take a moment to think about your answers and rate your responses on a 5-point scale, where 5 equals "excellent" and 1 equals "very poor." Then tally up your scores, and go to the categories at the bottom of the next page to see how you did.

1. You get a new cell phone. How long does it take you to remember the number? Give yourself a 1 if you have to check the phone every time you want to give out the number and a 5 if you know it by heart the next day.

1   2   3   4   5

2. How good are you at remembering where you put things? Give yourself a 5 if you never lose anything but a 1 if you have to search for the keys every time you want to leave the house.

1   2   3   4   5

3. You have a busy work day that you've carefully planned around a doctor's appointment. At the last minute, the doctor's office calls and asks you to reschedule your appointment from afternoon to morning. How good are you at juggling your plans to accommodate this change?

1   2   3   4   5

4. You're taking a trip back to your hometown and have several old friends to see, as well as old haunts to visit. You'll only be there for three days. How good are you at planning your visit so you can accomplish everything?

1   2   3   4   5

5. A friend takes you to a movie, and the next morning a curious coworker wants to hear the plot in depth. How good are you at remembering all the details?

1   2   3   4   5

6. Consider this scenario: You're brokering an agreement between two parties (could be anything from a business merger to making peace between feuding siblings), and both parties keep changing their demands. How good are you at adapting to the changing situation?

1   2   3   4   5

7. You're cooking a big meal for a family celebration. Say you have to cook everything—appetizers, entrees, sides, and desserts—all on the same day. How good are you at planning out each recipe so that everything is done and you can sit down and enjoy the meal with your family?

1   2   3   4   5

8. In an emotionally charged situation (for example, when you're giving a toast), can you usually come up with the right words to describe your feelings?

1   2   3   4   5

9. You and five friends have made a vow to always spend a certain amount of money on each other for holiday gifts. How good are you at calculating the prices of things in your head to make sure you spend the right amount of money?

1   2   3   4   5

10. You're moving, and you have to coordinate all the details of packing, hiring movers, cutting off and setting up utilities, and a hundred other small details. How good are you at planning out this complex situation?

1   2   3   4   5

10–25 Points: Are You Ready to Make a Change?
Remember, it's never too late to improve your brain health! A great way to start is to work puzzles each day, and you've taken the first step by buying this book. Choose a different type of puzzle each day, or do a variety of them to help strengthen memory, focus attention, and improve logic and problem-solving.

26–40 Points: Building Your Mental Muscles
You're no mental slouch, but there's always room to sharpen your mind! Choose puzzles that will challenge you, especially the types of puzzles you might not like as much or wouldn't normally do. Remember, doing a puzzle can be the mental equivalent of doing lunges or squats: While they might not be your first choice of activities, you'll definitely like the results!

41–50 Points: View from the Top
Congratulations! You're keeping your brain in tip-top shape. To maintain this level of mental fitness, keep challenging yourself by working puzzles every day. Like the rest of the body's muscles, your mental strength can decline if you don't use it. So choose to keep your brain supple and strong. You're at the summit, now you just have to stay to enjoy the view!

ANSWERS

Ace It! (page 11)

Grace, a certified hypochondriac, envisioned a day when she could go anyplace without a sick look on her face. Grace aced college but didn't get an MBA, ceasing her studies when she met Chase, a cerebral student of crustaceans who loved to look at her face and embrace her curvaceous figure. Being a recovering hypochondriac enabled Chase to relate to Grace, and he helped her recover by sharing his favorite placebo.

Math Grid (page 11)

			7
2	8	1	11
5	4	3	12
2	8	1	11
9	20	5	7

Tut's Tomb (page 12)

Wacky Wordy (page 12)

Play above the rim (a basketball term)

Sudoku (page 13)

8	2	6	1	7	5	4	3	9
7	4	3	2	9	6	8	1	5
9	1	5	4	3	8	6	7	2
6	8	4	9	5	3	7	2	1
3	7	2	6	1	4	9	5	8
5	9	1	7	8	2	3	6	4
1	6	8	5	4	7	2	9	3
4	5	7	3	2	9	1	8	6
2	3	9	8	6	1	5	4	7

Name Calling (page 14)

world's

Hinky Pinky (page 14)

1. right height; 2. leave Eve; 3. jarred guard;
4. yacht cot; 5. Hubbard blubbered

Acrostic Anagram (page 15)

A. cabin; B. symphonic; C. level; D. typing;
E. warhead; F. pecan; G. finalize; H. chore;
I. aviator; J. wearily; K. booze; L. output
"People who cannot recognize a palpable absurdity are very much in the way of civilization."
—Agnes Repplier

At the Zoo (page 16)

R	A	E	B	Z	G	A	Z	E	L	L	E	G
E	G	S	O	R	E	C	O	N	I	H	R	O
H	I	P	P	O	P	O	T	A	M	U	S	R
T	R	L	A	J	X	E	A	O	E	U	N	I
N	A	I	W	N	A	N	N	N	A	A	L	L
A	F	O	O	G	D	K	Y	G	E	N	K	A
P	F	N	L	T	E	A	T	L	U	Y	E	A
E	E	F	Y	W	A	C	A	M	I	H	D
R	E	G	I	T	E	L	E	P	H	A	N	T

Sudoku (page 17)

6	8	1	5	2	3	7	4	9
9	2	5	8	7	4	6	1	3
3	7	4	9	6	1	2	5	8
5	9	8	3	1	6	4	7	2
7	6	3	2	4	5	8	9	1
1	4	2	7	9	8	5	3	6
4	1	7	6	8	9	3	2	5
8	3	9	4	5	2	1	6	7
2	5	6	1	3	7	9	8	4

Word Ladders (page 17)

Answers may vary.
1. FOND, find, hind, hand, wand, wane, wine, mine, MINT
2. HOPE, hole, vole, vile, rile, ripe, ROPE

Answers

Crossword for Dummies (pages 18–19)

Name Calling (page 20)
course

Three-Letter Anagrams (page 20)
1. may/yam; 2. tub/but; 3. was/saw; 4. who/how;
5. not/ton

Big Top Code-doku (page 21)

Hidden message: SWALLOWER SWALLOWS
SEVERAL SWORDS

Wacky Wordy (page 21)
Blue in the face

Hinky Pinky (page 22)
1. pawn fawn; 2. bright knight; 3. castle hassle;
4. mean queen; 5. bring King
Theme: Chess pieces

All Hands on Deck (page 22)
Amy was wearing a watch with hour, minute, and
second hands. Betty was wearing a watch with
hour and minute hands. Carol was wearing a
digital watch with no hands.

Screwprint: Upside Down? (page 23)
Answer E is correct.

Crossword Snack (page 24)

Wacky Wordy (page 24)
One thing after another

Acrostic Anagram (page 25)
A. iodine; B. flowery; C. furious; D. wispy;
E. country; F. school; G. nominee; H. snore;
I. tornado; J. siege; K. reunion; L. shiny
"Writing is the only profession where no one
considers you ridiculous if you earn no money."
—Jules Renard

Sudoku (page 26)

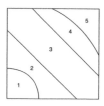

Wacky Wordy (page 26)
Empty promises

Squarely Put Together (page 27)

Wacky Wordy (page 27)
Change in the weather

Name Calling (page 28)
future

Word Ladders (page 28)
Answers may vary.
1. PEACH, teach, beach, beech, LEECH
2. SHOW, slow, flow, plow, prow, prop, DROP

172

Hinky Pinky (page 29)
1. split pit; 2. neat street; 3. built stilt;
4. tight fight; 5. eight straight
Theme: All 10 answer words end in T.

Circle Maze (page 30)

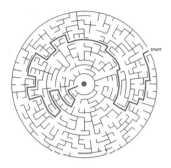

Weather Word Search (page 31)

```
F M D S L E E T F
A R L U N T T O A
H E O N W O H D I
C D C S C O W A R
L I G H T N I N G
O M O I N I N R O
U U O N C A D O F
D H R E M R O T S
```

Crossword Snack (page 32)

```
D R I B S
Y A H O O
I V A N A
N E V E R
G L E S S
```

Don't Lose Your Head! (page 32)
Sleepy Hollow

Cool Café (page 33)

	Surname	Drink	Sugar lumps
1	Dribble	latte	1
2	Aviary	coffee	2
3	Crumple	mocha	0
4	Bloggs	tea	3

Girls' Names Letter Box (page 34)

1	2	3	4	5	6	7	8	9	10	11	12	13
J	X	K	Z	B	S	H	Q	W	F	P	G	U
14	15	16	17	18	19	20	21	22	23	24	25	26
Y	D	V	E	R	O	N	I	C	A	L	T	M

Crossword Snack (page 35)

```
T A C I T
O P I N E
F I V E S
F L I R T
S E C T S
```

Garbage Bag (page 35)
Gabby bagged scraps of garbage in a plastic bag and dragged them to the curb aggressively, hoping to grab a glimpse of the cute garbage man, Bob, a guy with a lot of baggage who played bagpipes and was a rumba guru. At the curb, a gust of wind knocked Gabby over and gave her lumbago. Gabby knew she'd never dance the rumba again but hoped to make Bob agog with her homemade baguettes. Bob, aghast at the sight of Gabby on the curb, agreed to grab dinner after grabbing her arm and bringing her back to the garbage truck.

Jigshape (page 36)

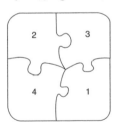

Wacky Wordy (page 36)
Get in shape

Crossword Snack (page 37)

```
G I T G O
O N E U P
U N H A T
R E E V E
D R E A D
```

Wacky Wordy (page 37)
An inside straight

Answers

Honeycomb Maze (page 38)

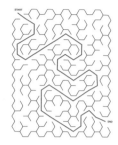

Friendly Pickup (page 39)

No matter how many businesses are on the street, Speedy made the pickups at 8 more businesses than Pokey.

(If the number of businesses on each side of the street is X, Speedy picks up X - 5 + 9 or X + 4, while Pokey picks up at 5 + X - 9 or X - 4, making the difference 8.)

Wacky Wordy (page 39)

End-over-end kick (football term)

Magazine Rack (page 40)

YELTSIN = INSTYLE
QUERIES = ESQUIRE
ORAL GUM = GLAMOUR
TEN-FOUR = FORTUNE
RATIFY IVAN = VANITY FAIR
ORLON SNIGLET = ROLLING STONE

Missing Connections (page 41)

Wacky Wordy (page 41)

Made in China

Lost in the Pentagon (page 42)

Remember Me? (Parts I and II) (pages 43–44)

Flames, Gargoyle, Hot Dog, Balloons, Acorns, Scarecrow, Decoys

Math Grid (page 44)

				15
7	2	6	1	16
1	3	4	2	10
3	2	2	5	12
8	3	1	4	16
19	10	13	12	16

Acrostic Anagram (page 45)

A. anyway; B. arctic; C. watery; D. tower;
E. chain; F. annoys; G. ozone; H. utility;
I. heaved; J. flank; K. layout; L. vivid

"You can't say that civilization don't advance . . . for in every war they kill you a new way."

—Will Rogers

Figuring Fast Food (page 46)

$2.75. If a burger and fries cost $3.50, and a small drink and cookie cost $1.50, then all four cost a total of $5. Take away the fries and small drink, which cost $2.25, and the remaining burger and cookie cost $2.75.

Boingo Wrapo (page 47)

The answer is F.

Hinky Pinky (page 48)

1. eats beets; 2. iPod tripod; 3. ending blending; 4. injure Ginger; 5. oak joke

Theme: The first letters of the answer words in order are E-I-E-I-O, the refrain in the children's song that begins "Old MacDonald Had a Farm."

Sudoku (page 48)

9	1	3	5	6	7	8	2	4
8	7	2	1	4	9	5	6	3
5	6	4	2	8	3	1	7	9
2	4	8	9	5	6	7	3	1
6	9	7	8	3	1	4	5	2
1	3	5	4	7	2	6	9	8
4	5	6	3	2	8	9	1	7
7	2	9	6	1	4	3	8	5
3	8	1	7	9	5	2	4	6

On Your Head (page 49)

F	W	A	R	T	S	H	E	L	M	E	T
E	D	R	O	N	O	S	T	E	T	S	X
D	O	Y	G	M	M	T	L	E	F	P	O
O	O	T	B	E	B	E	A	N	Y	A	B
R	H	U	A	R	R	E	Z	W	R	N	L
A	R	R	I	P	E	K	R	E	D	Á	L
G	Y	B	N	E	R	D	A	E	F	M	I
L	P	A	C	L	O	C	H	E	T	A	P
B	O	N	N	E	T	R	E	P	P	O	T

Venomous (pages 50–51)

B	I	B		T	A	B		O	A	T	E	R
U	S	A		A	L	A		N	U	R	S	E
L	A	N		J	E	L	L	Y	F	I	S	H
B	A	J	A		X	B	O	X		V	E	E
S	C	O	R	P	I	O	N		G	I	N	A
			R	O	S	A		T	R	A	C	T
S	A	R	I	S				M	U	L	E	S
P	R	O	V	E		S	C	A	N			
E	A	S	E		S	T	I	N	G	R	A	Y
A	B	A		S	O	A	R		E	A	V	E
K	I	N	G	C	O	B	R	A		B	A	N
T	A	N	Y	A		L	U	G		B	I	T
O	N	E	P	M		E	S	E		I	L	L

Four-Letter Anagrams (page 52)

1. live/evil; 2. Emil/lime; 3. much/chum;
4. love/vole; 5. alit/tail; 6. said/dais; 7. sore/rose;
8. read/dear; 9. balm/lamb; 10. time/emit

Math Grid (page 52)

						27
2	3	5	4	1	7	22
2	3	1	4	3	6	19
6	9	8	7	8	1	39
1	2	5	3	4	2	17
4	2	3	6	7	5	27
3	2	1	6	3	4	19

18 21 23 30 26 25 27

Black Hole Maze (page 53)

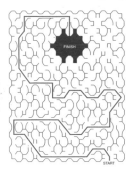

Acrostic Anagram (page 54)

A. catamaran; B. thereabout; C. leaflet;
D. succumb; E. bench; F. facade; G. haggle;
H. convergence; I. telephone; J. hyphen
"Change the changeable, accept the unchange-
able, and remove yourself from the unacceptable."
—Denis Waitley

Name Calling (page 55)

underestimate

Can You Find It? (page 55)

Jeff indicated he found a lot of stuff in Dallas
when he left Flint indiscreetly to work as
a pathfinder with the deaf Indian he met while
searching for some kind of indigo-colored
staff in desolate corners of town. A refined
fisherman who felt stiff indoors, Jeff fried a fish
he caught and had the fin delivered to a friend
in Flint, a buff inductee in the Finnish air force
named Findley. Finding himself in dire need of
funds, Findley sold the fin despite warnings from
Jeff indicating it would put his life in disarray.

Answers

Jigshape (page 56)

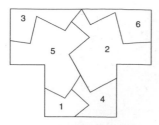

Missing Connections (page 57)

Holiday Anagram (page 57)
German/manger

Word Columns (page 58)
Often I get the feeling the whole world is against me, but deep down I know that's not true. Some smaller countries are neutral.

What a Racket (page 58)
M
Game, Set, Match

Screwprint: Criss-Cross (page 59)
Answer D is correct.

Sudoku (page 60)

6	1	2	5	4	8	7	3	9
5	8	9	7	3	1	2	6	4
3	4	7	6	2	9	5	1	8
7	6	1	9	5	3	8	4	2
2	3	4	1	8	7	6	9	5
9	5	8	2	6	4	1	7	3
1	2	6	3	9	5	4	8	7
8	7	3	4	1	2	9	5	6
4	9	5	8	7	6	3	2	1

Crypto-Game Families (page 61)
1. basketball, polo, golf, croquet, volleyball, tennis, football, bocce, baseball, soccer
2. bridge, euchre, pinochle, canasta, gin rummy, crazy eights, poker, hearts, solitaire, baccarat
3. chess, Scrabble, checkers, Monopoly, Battleship, Game of Life, Chinese checkers, Parcheesi, Clue, Sorry

Poker Logic (page 62)
Ace Grace's husband is Trey.
The order (clockwise) was Trey, Queenie, King, Ace Grace, Jack, Wild Winnie.

Word Ladders (page 62)
Answers may vary.
1. SWEAT, sweet, sheet, sheer, steer, STEEP
2. MANOR, minor, miner, miser, wiser, WIPER

Mythology Letter Box (page 63)

1	2	3	4	5	6	7	8	9	10	11	12	13
H	E	R	A	D	S	Z	F	L	J	U	N	O

14	15	16	17	18	19	20	21	22	23	24	25	26
G	I	V	T	B	X	C	K	Y	M	P	W	Q

Sudoku (page 64)

9	4	2	6	3	5	1	7	8
1	7	5	8	9	2	3	6	4
8	3	6	4	7	1	9	2	5
2	5	8	3	1	4	7	9	6
3	9	4	7	8	6	2	5	1
7	6	1	2	5	9	4	8	3
4	1	7	5	2	8	6	3	9
6	8	3	9	4	7	5	1	2
5	2	9	1	6	3	8	4	7

Out of the World Anagram (page 64)
meteor/remote

Acrostic Anagram (page 65)
A. trends; B. branded; C. clasps; D. bungler; E. honey; F. refine; G. rushing; H. morning; I. angry; J. disdain; K. details; L. orient
"Humor brings insight and tolerance. Irony brings a deeper and less friendly understanding."
—Agnes Repplier

Hinky Pinky (page 66)
1. girl's curls; 2. large charge; 3. Toto photo;
4. liking Viking; 5. imitation limitation

Name Calling (page 66)
giveth
taketh

Things You Shouldn't Touch (Parts I and II) (pages 67–68)
POISON-DART FROGS, ROADKILL, OLEANDER, TAINTED FOOD, RATTLESNAKES

It's a Gas! (page 68)
Helium. Substitute the letters of the alphabet for the corresponding numbers.

Math Grid (page 69)

				108
4	5	5	3	300
2	6	3	4	144
1	3	5	2	30
4	2	6	4	192

32 180 450 96 480

Name Calling (page 69)
Imagination

Feeding Time (page 70)

	Name	Food	Spoonfuls
1	Connie	rabbit	10
2	Bill	chicken	13
3	Des	beef	12
4	Alice	tuna	15

Name Calling (page 70)
manufacturers

Boys' Names Letter Box (page 71)

1	2	3	4	5	6	7	8	9	10	11	12	13
P	I	J	C	H	A	R	L	E	S	U	F	W

14	15	16	17	18	19	20	21	22	23	24	25	26
M	X	D	Q	B	K	Z	T	O	N	Y	G	V

Aphorism Code-doku (page 72)

C	T	F	R	H	A	S	I	E
A	E	H	S	F	I	C	R	T
I	R	S	T	E	C	F	H	A
H	S	T	I	C	F	A	E	R
E	I	C	H	A	R	T	F	S
F	A	R	E	S	T	I	C	H
R	F	A	C	T	E	H	S	I
T	H	E	F	I	S	R	A	C
S	C	I	A	R	H	E	T	F

Hidden message: THE FIRST CAT CATCHES THE RAT

Marital Anagram (page 72)
matrons/transom

Red, White, and Blue (page 73)

	A	B	C	D	E	F
1	R	R	W	B	W	B
2	W	W	B	R	R	B
3	B	R	B	W	R	W
4	W	B	R	W	B	R
5	R	W	R	B	B	W
6	B	B	W	R	W	R

Math Grid (page 74)

			30
6	1	3	18
4	5	6	120
2	6	4	48

48 30 72 120

Word Ladders (page 74)
Answers may vary.
1. IOTA, rota, rote, rate, pate, pale, pall, BALL
2. MEET, meat, beat, boat, goat, goad, TOAD

Crossword Snack (page 75)

G	R	A	D	E
L	O	V	E	D
A	M	O	N	G
R	A	I	S	E
E	N	D	E	D

Barefoot Logic (page 75)
Barefoot Bob has four socks in his drawer and they are any color but white, black, or brown.

Answers

Seeing Double (pages 76–77)

Clue answers: 1. BAD DOG; 2. C CLEF; 3. DO YOU UNDERSTAND?; 4. FOR REAL; 5. GAG GIFT; 6. GO OUT; 7. GRAB BAG; 8. GROW WEARY; 9. HALL OF FAME; 10. HIGH HOPES; 11. I INSIST; 12. IS SURE; 13. MARTIAL LAW; 14. MIDDLE EAST; 15. ROMAN NUMERAL; 16. SANTA ANA; 17. SAY YES; 18. SIT TIGHT; 19. SKIM MILK; 20. STEAK KNIFE; 21. STOP PAYMENT

Hidden message: In the big game, a quick kick hit a drum major on the goal line

World Cities Letter Box (page 78)

1	2	3	4	5	6	7	8	9	10	11	12	13
H	J	O	C	P	A	R	I	S	D	V	F	K

14	15	16	17	18	19	20	21	22	23	24	25	26
Q	Y	N	Z	E	U	T	B	X	M	G	W	L

Cube Crazy (page 79)

Figure D

Read Between the Lines (pages 80–81)

1. AMERICAN AIRLINES; 2. AQUILINE; 3. BASELINE; 4. BEELINE; 5. BEHIND ENEMY LINES; 6. BIKINI LINE; 7. CLEANLINESS; 8. DEADLINE; 9. DISCIPLINE; 10. DOTTED LINE; 11. EYELINER; 12. FUR-LINED; 13. GASOLINE; 14. HEMLINE; 15. HOTLINE; 16. "I WALK THE LINE"; 17. INLINE SKATING; 18. JAWLINE; 19. LANDLINE; 20. LINE DANCE; 21. LINE OF CREDIT; 22. LINEAGE; 23. LINEAR ALGEBRA; 24. LINEBACKER; 25. LINEN CLOSET; 26. MASCULINE; 27. MILLINER; 28. NECKLINE; 29. OCEAN LINER; 30. PATSY CLINE; 31. PICKET LINE; 32. PICK-UP LINE; 33. PUNCH LINE; 34. RECLINER; 35. SKYLINE; 36. STARTING LINEUP; 37. THE LINE FORMS HERE; 38. TIMELINE; 39. TRAMPOLINE; 40. UGLINESS

Hidden message: I draw the line when it comes to line drawings

Sudoku (page 82)

1	8	4	5	2	9	7	3	6
5	2	7	3	6	8	9	1	4
9	6	3	1	7	4	8	2	5
2	9	6	8	1	7	5	4	3
3	4	8	9	5	2	6	7	1
7	1	5	4	3	6	2	8	9
4	7	2	6	9	3	1	5	8
6	3	1	7	8	5	4	9	2
8	5	9	2	4	1	3	6	7

Ohio Anagram (page 82)

tooled, Toledo, looted

Crypto-Wisdom (page 83)

1. Worry is a misuse of the imagination.
2. The worst thing about mistakes in the kitchen is that you usually have to eat them.
3. Don't forget that appreciation is always appreciated.

Math Grid (page 83)

```
                              34
 3 6 5 8 9 1 2  34
 8 6 3 9 2 8 4  40
 7 2 8 5 4 4 5  35
 9 8 6 7 9 2 3  44
 7 1 6 4 2 5 6  31
 3 2 4 6 5 4 7  31
 5 2 3 4 6 7 1  28
 42 27 35 43 37 31 28 31
```

Star Power (page 84)

Medical Anagram (page 84)

sedative, deviates

Word Columns (page 85)

"The first man to compare the cheeks of a young woman to a rose was obviously a poet; the first to repeat it was possibly an idiot."

—Salvador Dali

Day at the Zoo (page 86)

Changes in second picture: 1. County is now Country; 2. flags are white; 3. extra post supporting zoo sign; 4. extra bush below sign; 5. child with balloons holding man's right hand; 6. tiger cage narrower; 7. only 1 tiger; 8. person in front of cage has back turned to tiger; 9. person in front of tiger cage is now a woman; 10. child walking has no cotton candy; 11. adult giraffe has no mane; 12. same giraffe gained an ear; 13. baby giraffe's spots are different; 14. less hay around baby giraffe; 15. bars missing from giraffe pen; 16. boy at giraffe pen wearing extra shirt; 17. girl taking photo has stripes on her shirt; 18. woman with stroller is wearing a hat; 19. same woman is now wearing a skirt; 20. child in stroller has 3 balloons; 21. only 1 boy is watching elephant; 22. no branch in elephant's trunk; 23. elephant's tusk is shorter; 24. elephant's trunk outside of fence.

Hinky Pinky (page 87)

1. blurrier furrier; 2. deduction reduction; 3. cavity gravity; 4. misspelling dispelling; 5. stadium radium

Cast-a-Word (page 87)

Die 1: A B S U V X
Die 2: C H I N Y Z
Die 3: D E F G K P
Die 4: L M O R T W

Word Jigsaw (page 88)

```
      O P T
C A M E O
A L E R T
T E N
```

Wacky Wordy (page 88)

Indigo (In DEE GO)

Missing Connections (page 89)

```
T R A V E L   A R C
  E   E   O   P   A
A N T E   U S I N G
  E   E   D   N   E
A W E D   E D G E R
D   E T S     A
V A M P   T R U T H
E   E       T   A
R   N O R M A   R
B O L D     H O P
```

Wacky Wordy (page 89)

Forty acres and a mule

Ball Games (pages 90–91)

```
T A B   L A M P   Y O K E
A L L   C L I O   E R O S
R O U N D E R S   M I S S
P E R E       I S E E
  T A B L E T E N N I S
    L O O N   N I T R O
P A C   N O D E S   S K Y
A M O C O   O L E O
L A W N B O W L I N G
  P O O R       T E A K
B O O T   L A C R O S S E
L U K E   O K A Y   T I L
T I E S   N A M E   S A P
```

Answers

Star Trek Maze (page 92)

Math Grid (page 93)

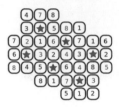

								27
7	4	5	1	2	9	2		30
3	8	5	4	3	6	1		30
2	6	5	9	4	7	7		40
6	5	4	8	7	5	6		41
9	8	3	7	1	4	5		37
2	1	8	4	2	4	4		25
3	6	6	5	3	5	3		31

32 38 36 38 22 40 28 36

Wacky Wordy (page 93)
Double-team coverage (football term)

Acrostic Anagram (page 94)
A. breathless; B. thermometer; C. foregoes;
D. fortify; E. euthanasia; F. faction; G. eunuch;
H. chunky; I. widowed
"More firm and sure the hand of courage strikes,
when it obeys the watchful eye of caution."
                                    —James Thomson

Hinky Pinky (page 95)
1. aisle pile; 2. choppy copy; 3. snail tale;
4. usher's gushers; 4. vandals' sandals

Witty Anagram (page 95)
epitaphs, happiest

Hurry! (pages 96–97)

S	T	A	B		A	L	P		S	L	E	W
O	H	I	O		L	E	E		N	A	P	E
D	O	N	T	W	A	I	T		A	K	I	N
A	U	T	H	O	R		A	S	P	E	C	T
				O	M	E	L	E	T			
G	U	A	R	D	E	D		C	O	H	O	S
U	G	L	I		D	I	M		I	O	W	A
T	H	I	G	H		C	O	A	T	I	N	G
	H	E	C	T	I	C						
B	I	S	T	R	O		S	T	A	T	U	S
E	D	E	N		L	E	T	S	R	O	L	L
T	O	R	O		A	G	E		E	D	N	A
S	L	A	W		S	O	N		A	D	A	M

Star Power (page 98)

(See grid)

Cat Logic (page 98)
Mr. Stripes owns Rusty.
Mr. Rusty owns Puddles.
Mr. Tommy owns Stripes.
Mr. Puddles owns Tommy.

Number Crossword (page 99)

4	9		
4	3	2	1
1	2	3	4
	5	4	

Math Grid (page 99)

					144
1	2	5	4	2	80
2	6	4	3	5	720
4	3	3	2	1	72
5	4	5	2	3	600
2	1	6	4	3	144

80 144 1800 192 90 108

Around Three Cubes (page 100)

Figures B and C match.

Acrostic Anagram (page 101)

A. acerbic; B. repetitive; C. gushes; D. entity;
E. overjoys; F. navigational; G. enviable;
H. belonged; I. follower

"If your job is to leaven ordinary lives with
elevating spectacle, be elevating or be gone."

—George F. Will

Sudoku (page 102)

7	6	9	4	3	1	5	8	2
4	1	5	2	6	8	9	7	3
3	8	2	5	7	9	6	4	1
8	9	3	7	1	6	4	2	5
5	2	1	9	4	3	8	6	7
6	4	7	8	5	2	1	3	9
1	5	6	3	8	7	2	9	4
2	3	4	6	9	5	7	1	8
9	7	8	1	2	4	3	5	6

Genius Anagram (page 102)

Einstein, nineties

Word Jigsaw (page 103)

Ageless Logic (page 103)

Grandma is 61.

Insect Marriages (page 104)

	Groom	Bride	Surname
1	cockroach	grasshopper	Loopy
2	ant	butterfly	Kent
3	earthworm	honeybee	Mags
4	dragonfly	wasp	Ozone
5	beetle	flea	Nomad

Things That Smell Good (Parts I and II) (pages 105–106)

GARLIC, JASMINE, ONIONS, CHOW
MEIN, LICORICE, CARAMEL
CORN, DOUGHNUTS, CHOCOLATE

Math Grid (page 106)

Red, White, and Blue (page 107)

	A	B	C	D	E	F
1	R	W	W	R	B	B
2	W	B	R	B	W	R
3	B	W	B	W	R	R
4	W	B	R	R	B	W
5	R	R	W	B	W	B
6	B	R	B	W	R	W

Aphorism Code-doku (page 108)

G	H	N	W	M	T	O	R	E
R	M	O	G	E	N	H	W	T
E	W	T	H	O	R	G	N	M
H	T	W	O	G	E	N	M	R
O	N	G	M	R	W	T	E	H
M	R	E	T	N	H	W	G	O
T	E	H	N	W	M	R	O	G
W	O	M	R	H	G	E	T	N
N	G	R	E	T	O	M	H	W

Hidden message: HERE NOW, GONE
TOMORROW

Word Ladders (page 108)

Answers may vary.
1. PLANT, plank, blank, blink, brink, brine,
   BRIDE
2. SANDY, dandy, candy, caddy, DADDY

The Castle of Horror (page 109)

Dracula. Going from left to right, the number
of merlons on each section of the castle's battle-
ments correspond with the positions of the letters of the alphabet in the word Dracula.

Answers

Math Grid (page 109)

					480
5	6	4	3	1	360
4	6	3	5	2	720
3	2	4	6	5	720
2	4	6	3	4	576
6	4	3	3	5	1080

720 1152 864 810 200 1800

Word Jigsaw (page 110)

```
G E M
N O O S E
U N D E R
    E A R
```

Timely Sequence (page 110)

P

Eastern, Central, Mountain, Pacific (four time zones)

Remember Me? (Parts I and II) (pages 111–112)

Easel, Ponytail, Tomahawk, Whale, Ears of corn, Backpack

Missing Connections (page 112)

```
D I Z Z Y   C R A M
E   E   E   A     A
P L A T T E R     N
E   L     O K A Y
N   V E A L   B
D O   E   B   L
    N   I N F E R
H O S T E D   A   E
A   A   E   N   A
M A Y O R   T S A R
```

Word Columns (page 113)

You should always try to keep a smile on your face and a melody in your heart. Once you master that, try patting your head and rubbing your belly at the same time.

Odd-Even Logidoku (page 114)

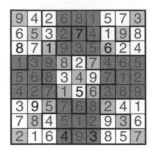

```
9 4 2 6 8 1 5 7 3
6 5 3 2 7 4 1 9 8
8 7 1 9 3 5 6 2 4
1 3 9 8 2 7 4 6 5
5 6 8 3 4 9 7 1 2
4 2 7 1 5 6 3 8 9
3 9 5 7 6 8 2 4 1
7 8 4 5 1 2 9 3 6
2 1 6 4 9 3 8 5 7
```

Cast-a-Word (page 114)

Die 1: A H J T W Z
Die 2: B G K L O U
Die 3: C F I M R S
Die 4: D E N P Q Y

Supermarket Sojourn (page 115)

Occupation Word Search (page 116)

Eleven Coins (page 117)

Put 3 coins in each pan. If they balance, then all are true coins. Then put 5 of them against the 5 not used to see which is heaviest.

If there is not a balance from the first weighing, then the excluded 5 coins are true. Balance 3 of these against the heavy group of 3 coins from the first weighing to determine if the fake is heavier or lighter than a true coin.

Star Power (page 117)

Famous Fare (pages 118–119)

S	L	O	W		P	I	P	E		M	A	C	E	S
C	U	B	E		A	D	E	N		E	L	E	N	A
O	N	E	A		L	E	N	D		S	O	L	O	N
R	A	Y	R	O	M	A	N	O	C	H	E	E	S	E
E	R	S		M	E	L			H	E	S	S		
			B	A	R		A	P	E	S		T	W	A
O	F	T	E	N		A	C	R	E		S	I	A	M
M	A	R	T	I	N	S	H	O	R	T	C	A	K	E
I	C	E	S		A	H	E	M		H	O	L	E	S
T	E	A		A	B	E	D		C	U	T			
		T	R	I	O		S	A	M		S	A	T	
J	A	M	E	S	B	R	O	W	N	B	E	T	T	Y
A	R	E	A	L		O	P	E	N		C	O	O	P
M	I	N	C	E		W	A	D	E		H	O	N	E
B	A	T	H	S		S	L	E	D		O	D	E	S

Granola Logic (page 120)

39 cents per ounce means a pound costs $6.24.
oats: 10 ounces ($3.60)
raisins: 3 ounces ($1.29)
almonds: 3 ounces ($1.35)

Logidoku (page 120)

8	2	3	9	7	5	4	6	1
5	6	1	4	3	2	7	9	8
7	9	4	8	6	1	5	3	2
4	7	9	1	5	8	6	2	3
3	8	5	6	2	7	9	1	4
2	1	6	3	4	9	8	7	5
1	5	7	2	8	6	3	4	9
9	4	8	7	1	3	2	5	6
6	3	2	5	9	4	1	8	7

Holiday Anagram (page 121)

1. thread; 2. handy; 3. Andes; 4. nacre; 5. kayoed; 6. smiled; 7. garden; 8. inlets; 9. volley; 10. inane; 11. nectar; 12. garnet

U.S. holiday: Thanksgiving

Big Screen Letter Box (page 122)

| 1 | 2 | 3 | 4 | 5 | 6 | 7 | 8 | 9 | 10 | 11 | 12 | 13 |
| M | X | N | S | J | O | L | I | E | V | A | W | F |

| 14 | 15 | 16 | 17 | 18 | 19 | 20 | 21 | 22 | 23 | 24 | 25 | 26 |
| Y | B | T | P | G | C | R | U | Z | H | D | Q | K |

Magic Square (page 123)

17	24	1	8	15
23	5	7	14	16
4	6	13	20	22
10	12	19	21	3
11	18	25	2	9

Crypto-Quote (page 123)

"There are two things that are more difficult than making an after-dinner speech: Climbing a wall which is leaning toward you and kissing a girl who is leaning away from you."

—Winston Churchill

Word Columns (page 124)

After eating an entire bull, a mountain lion felt so good he started roaring. He kept it up until a hunter came along and shot him. The moral: When you're full of bull, keep your mouth shut.

Answers

Letter Quilt (page 125)

A	D	C			B
B	C			D	A
D		B	A		C
A		C	D	B	
C	B			A	D
	D	A	B	C	

Word Ladders (page 125)

Answers may vary.

1. RIVET, river, rover, rower, bower, bowel, TOWEL
2. BADGER, bagger, dagger, danger, manger, manner, BANNER

Mirror, Mirror (page 126)

1. Wallpaper different; 2. mirror frame different; 3. page taped to mirror reads "hair"; 4. necklace hanging on mirror changed from circle to heart; 5. roses changed to daisies; 6. bottle on tray missing; 7. jar in front of vase moved back; 8. perfume bottle changed shape; 9. drawer opened; 10. necklace on table disappeared; 11. table legs changed; 12. hair in reflection different; 13. now wearing necklace; 14. sleeves appeared; 15. belt ties appeared; 16. chair pad grew ruffles; 17. shoe different; 18. a slipper disappeared; 19. wallpaper goes to floor; 20. now wearing ring; 21. purse fell over; 22. bangs in picture different

Acrostic Anagram (page 127)

A. incapacitated; B. perished; C. usefulness; D. survey; E. forehead; F. fishing; G. witting; H. willow; I. sorority

"Virtue is its own reward. There's a pleasure in doing good which sufficiently pays itself."
—Sir John Vanbrugh

ABCD (page 128)

A	2	2	1	1	1	2	
B	2	0	2	3	1	1	
C	1	1	2	0	3	2	
A B C D	1	3	1	2	1	1	

2	0	1	3	D	A	D	A	D	C
1	1	3	1	C	D	C	B	C	A
1	3	1	1	B	A	B	D	B	C
3	1	1	1	A	D	A	B	C	A
1	2	1	2	B	C	B	D	A	D
1	2	2	1	A	D	C	B	C	B

Wacky Wordies (page 128)

1. Mixed nuts
2. Three up, three down (baseball term)

Flower Garden Word Search (page 129)

A gardener needs sunshine, water, good soil, fertilizer, and a very sharp hoe!

Letter Quilt (page 130)

A	D	C		B	
B			D	C	A
C		B	A		D
	A		C	D	B
	B	D		A	C
D	C	A	B		

184

Star Power (page 130)

TV Documentaries (page 131)

	First word	Second word	Director
1	Stealing	Money	Spoolbag
2	Cutting	Bread	Alhen
3	Painting	Newspapers	Rodrigo
4	Eating	Cloth	Torrentino
5	Ripping	Wallpaper	Jockson
6	Making	Pizza	Capri

Not in the Dairy Case (pages 132–133)

Euphemism Anagram (page 134)

OHIO EMBLEM = MOBILE HOME
RED TUNES = DENTURES
PROVIDENCE WHEEL = PREOWNED
    VEHICLE
BLUE MINNESOTAN = UNMENTIONABLES
ALL TIN FAIRYLANDS = SANITARY
    LANDFILL
FICTIONAL CAROLER CITY =
    CORRECTIONAL FACILITY
VIDEO MUTANT = UNMOTIVATED
OPEN AIRSTRIP = PERSPIRATION
TIN COIN SEIZER = SENIOR CITIZEN
BOISTEROUS MATH = BATHROOM TISSUE
LOBOTOMY LISTER = LITTLE BOYS'
    ROOM

Math Grid (page 135)

						16
5	1	4	3	4	2	480
3	2	5	4	1	4	480
4	4	3	1	2	2	192
2	3	4	2	6	1	288
1	2	4	5	3	3	360
1	5	3	2	1	4	120
120	240	2880	240	144	192	720

Word Ladders (page 135)

Answers may vary.
1. CLUSTER, bluster, blaster, plaster, platter, PLANTER
2. GREAT, treat, tread, bread, breed, greed, GREET

Anagram Place (page 136)

1. runway/unwary; 2. otter/torte; 3. cheap/peach;
4. kilns/slink; 5. yodel/Doyle; 6. manor/roman;
7. onset/stone; 8. unseat/Austen; 9. Notre/tenor;
10. tiara/riata; 11. attic/tacit; 12. icers/cries;
13. napped/append; 14. snake/sneak
U.S. location: Rocky Mountains

Good-Looking Logic (page 137)

Johnny Pitt installed his global positioning
    system in his attic.
George Cruise installed a robot vacuum in his
    living room.
Tom Depp installed a PC in his bathroom.
Brad Damon installed a wide-screen TV in his
    bedroom.
Matt Clooney installed a DVD player in his
    kitchen.

Acrostic Anagram (page 138)

A. counterbalance; B. dossier; C. goldfish;
D. thornier; E. heartaches; F. thereafter;
G. wafts; H. venue; I. without
"A hurtful act is the transference to others of the
degradation which we bear in ourselves."
    —Simone Weil

Answers

Red, White, and Blue (page 139)

	A	B	C	D	E	F
1	R	B	B	W	R	W
2	B	B	W	R	W	R
3	R	W	W	B	R	B
4	W	R	R	B	B	W
5	W	R	B	R	W	B
6	B	W	R	W	B	R

Big Top Code-doku (page 140)

N	S	M	O	L	I	A	E	T
E	A	I	S	M	T	N	O	L
O	L	T	N	A	E	M	I	S
L	E	N	A	T	S	O	M	I
S	I	O	M	N	L	E	T	A
T	M	A	E	I	O	S	L	N
M	O	L	T	S	A	I	N	E
I	N	S	L	E	M	T	A	O
A	T	E	I	O	N	L	S	M

Hidden message: MAN ON A MISSION TAMES NINE LIONS

Puzzling Series (page 140)

Just add a line to each of the letters **P**, **T**, and **F** to get **R**, **I**, and **E** and the word SERIES!

Living Large Anagram (page 141)

HOT GAIL = GOLIATH
THE PLANE = ELEPHANT
CNN TONITE = CONTINENT
OSTRICH MELT = STRETCH LIMO
LEO MUSIC = COLISEUM
SUSIE CHIRP = CRUISE SHIP
NO EMOLLIENT FLAB = FOOTBALL LINEMEN
MEOW RUSTLERS = SUMO WRESTLER
NANCY DRAGON = GRAND CANYON
END BATTALION = NATIONAL DEBT

U.S. Presidents Letter Box (page 142)

1	2	3	4	5	6	7	8	9	10	11	12	13
V	N	J	T	A	Y	L	O	R	C	F	I	P

14	15	16	17	18	19	20	21	22	23	24	25	26
M	W	Q	G	D	B	U	S	H	K	X	E	Z

Nice Pets (page 143)

	Owner	Pet	Name
1	Arthur	pig	Norma
2	Cathy	cat	Len
3	Evelyn	crocodile	Keith
4	Bob	rhino	Olive
5	Dennis	leopard	Molly

Math Grid (page 144)

1	5	3	6	7	4	9	7	8	50
4	2	7	4	3	5	6	6	9	46
9	8	3	7	1	5	4	2	7	46
8	3	4	4	2	3	5	5	9	43
1	9	3	2	7	2	6	7	8	45
8	2	5	4	3	9	9	4	5	49
7	6	3	9	3	7	8	1	4	48
2	4	9	8	2	1	3	2	9	40
9	8	3	7	4	6	8	5	3	53

48 (top)
49 47 40 51 32 42 58 39 62 39

Wacky Wordy (page 144)

Add 'em up

Painterly Logic (page 145)

Trailer 101: violet roof, orange doors, indigo walls
Trailer 102: red roof, blue doors, yellow walls
Trailer 103: green roof, yellow doors, red walls
Trailer 104: indigo roof, green doors, violet walls
Trailer 105: blue roof, red doors, orange walls

Herbs and Spices (page 146)

AACHEN ICE = ECHINACEA
HARD PEE = EPHEDRA
EGGS INN = GINSENG
RAN ALIVE = VALERIAN
MY FORCE = COMFREY
MAD KAREN = MANDRAKE
NEHRU HOOD = HOREHOUND
CLAIM HOME = CHAMOMILE
NATIONAL DEED = DANDELION TEA

Logidoku (page 147)

5	3	6	4	9	8	7	2	1
9	1	7	5	2	3	8	6	4
2	4	8	7	6	1	9	5	3
8	7	4	6	1	2	5	3	9
3	5	2	8	7	9	1	4	6
1	6	9	3	5	4	2	8	7
6	2	5	9	4	7	3	1	8
7	8	1	2	3	6	4	9	5
4	9	3	1	8	5	6	7	2

Genius Logic (page 147)

Two. The secret code was to reply to the doorman with the number of words he said to you.

Math Grid (page 148)

										72
3	4	7	7	5	6	8	1	9	7	57
3	6	7	5	6	9	5	9	8	6	64
4	5	8	7	9	8	5	7	6	2	61
6	8	4	6	4	7	9	9	6	5	64
9	5	6	8	7	6	2	8	4	9	64
2	7	8	3	9	5	3	9	7	5	58
6	5	8	9	3	4	7	2	9	4	57
4	5	7	6	8	3	5	9	7	1	55
8	7	5	9	6	2	5	3	8	9	62
3	9	7	5	6	1	6	5	4	3	49
48	61	67	65	63	51	55	62	68	51	62

Crypto-Quote (page 148)

"The first and most important thing of all, at least for writers today, is to strip language clean, to lay it bare down to the bone."

—Ernest Hemingway

Oh, Waiter! (page 149)

Tree Tops (pages 150–151)

Acrostic Anagram (page 152)

A. preparedness; B. flophouses; C. motions; D. pontoon; E. adaptation; F. forehead; G. ravenously; H. diffused

"To depend upon a profession is a less odious form of slavery than to depend upon a father."

—Virginia Woolf

Answers

Star Power (page 153)

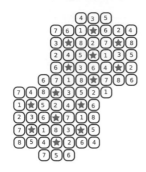

Word Jigsaw (page 154)

Move It! (page 154)

Move the line in the letter Q to the P, to create BRAVO

Hashi (page 155)

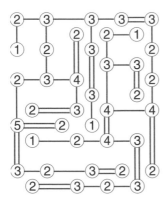

Number Crossword (page 155)

Big Top Code-doku (page 156)

H	D	R	C	Y	P	M	A	E
C	A	M	E	D	H	R	Y	P
Y	E	P	M	R	A	C	H	D
D	M	C	H	E	R	Y	P	A
P	H	A	Y	C	D	E	R	M
R	Y	E	A	P	M	H	D	C
A	C	Y	D	H	E	P	M	R
E	P	D	R	M	Y	A	C	H
M	R	H	P	A	C	D	E	Y

Hidden message: A CAMPY PACHYDERM PARADE

Word Ladders (page 156)

Answers may vary.
1. RHYME, thyme, Thame, shame, shake, stake, stale, STALL
2. GRIME, crime, clime, slime, slide, snide, snipe, SWIPE

Wild West (page 157)

	Name	Surname	Location	Firearm
1	Abel	Garrett	Fort Griffin	Cavalry
2	Drew	Indiana	San Antonio	Peacemaker
3	Earp	James	Red River	Schofield
4	Fingers	Hitchcock	Dodge City	Winchester
5	Butch	Lightning	Colby	Golden Boy
6	Cat	Kid	Ogallala	Derringer

Fitting Words (page 158)

T	A	B	L	E
A	G	L	O	W
C	O	U	P	E
O	G	R	E	S

Cross Math (page 158)

7	+	6	-	3	=	10
+		-		-		
5	+	4	+	1	=	10
-		+		+		
2	x	9	-	8	=	10
=		=		=		
10		11		10		

Red, White, Blue, and Green (page 159)

	A	B	C	D	E	F	G	H
1	B	W	R	W	G	B	G	R
2	G	W	R	B	G	R	W	B
3	R	G	G	B	W	W	B	R
4	W	R	B	R	B	G	G	W
5	R	B	W	G	R	W	B	G
6	W	B	B	G	R	G	R	W
7	B	R	G	R	W	B	W	G
8	G	G	W	W	B	R	R	B

Acrostic Anagram (page 160)

A. macabre; B. anthrax; C. whammed;
D. westerns; E. thinnest; F. cataracts;
G. alarmists; H. hotheaded; I. hoodwinks
"The world embarrasses me, and I cannot dream
that this watch exists and has no watchmaker."
—Voltaire

Word Jigsaw (page 161)

Star Power (page 162)

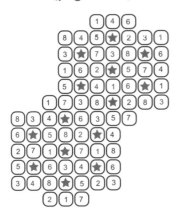

Hashi (page 163)

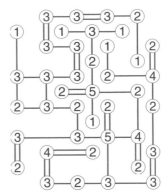

Cross Math (page 163)

5	+	9	÷	7	=	2
-		-		+		
8	x	1	x	3	=	24
+		-		x		
6	-	4	+	2	=	4
=		=		=		
3		4		20		

Word Columns (page 164)

"Not every truth is the better for showing its face
undisguised and often silence is the wisest thing
for a man to heed."
—Pindar

Wacky Wordy (page 164)

A little goes a long way

Logidoku (page 165)

8	6	5	7	2	1	9	4	3
4	9	2	5	3	8	1	7	6
1	3	7	6	9	4	2	8	5
9	8	6	2	4	5	7	3	1
7	5	3	8	1	6	4	9	2
2	1	4	9	7	3	6	5	8
3	2	8	4	6	7	5	1	9
5	4	9	1	8	2	3	6	7
6	7	1	3	5	9	8	2	4

Answers

Fitting Words (page 165)

```
Q U A S H
U N T I E
A D O R N
D O P E S
```

Prize Poetry (page 166)

	Name	Surname	State	Poem
1	Francis	Grimble	Nebraska	Waterfall
2	Daisy	Irvine	Ohio	Vanity
3	Betty	Lee	Montana	Sunrise
4	Andrea	Horse	Iowa	Umbrella
5	Erwin	Jackson	Pennsylvania	Tolerance
6	Colin	Keats	Colorado	Expectancy

Word Jigsaw (page 167)

```
    U S E
B A R E R
O W N E R
Y E S
```

The Start of Things (page 167)
H
In the beginning, God created the heaven and the earth

Aphorism Code-doku (page 168)

Hidden message: NAUGHT SOUGHT, NAUGHT CAUGHT

Hashi (page 168)

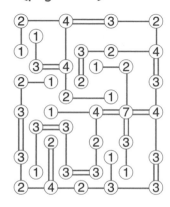

190

Index

continued on page 192